Undergraduate Topics in Computer Science

Undergraduate Topics in Computer Science (UTiCS) delivers high-quality instructional content for undergraduates studying in all areas of computing and information science. From core foundational and theoretical material to final-year topics and applications, UTiCS books take a fresh, concise, and modern approach and are ideal for self-study or for a one- or two-semester course. The texts are all authored by established experts in their fields, reviewed by an international advisory board, and contain numerous examples and problems. Many include fully worked solutions.

For other volumes:
http://www.springer.com/series/7592

Dan Chalmers

Sensing and Systems in Pervasive Computing

Engineering Context Aware Systems

Dan Chalmers
University of Sussex
Brighton
United Kingdom
D.Chalmers@sussex.ac.uk

ISSN 1863-7310
ISBN 978-0-85729-840-9   e-ISBN 978-0-85729-841-6
DOI 10.1007/978-0-85729-841-6
Springer London Dordrecht Heidelberg New York

British Library Cataloguing in Publication Data
A catalogue record for this book is available from the British Library

Library of Congress Control Number: 2011934743

Springer is part of Springer Science+Business Media (www.springer.com)

Preface

Audience

This book is designed to accompany a final year undergraduate or masters level course in *pervasive computing*, although it could serve well as a course for introducing sensors or experiment design to students in earlier years at university with some skimming over the research focus; or equally as a getting-started guide for PhD level students tacking pervasive computing, in particular programming sensors and context awareness, for the first time.

Book Approach and Structure

This book is about sensing and systems issues in pervasive computing. The reader may also be interested in the HCI issues, programming for Java J2ME, iOS, or Android—each of which would require a separate book; similarly for issues in wireless networks, sensor networks, embedded systems design etc we give an introductory coverage but other books should be consulted for deeper understanding of these topics. The approach of the book organises into three main parts and some supporting material: First we have an introductory chapter, introducing some of the issues and ideas and a discussion of experimental practise. In Part II we discuss some of the challenges raised by pervasive computing—in the limitations and variation of hardware and networks; and some of the tools being applied in pervasive computing—sensor devices, PDAs and mobile phones, wireless networks. In Part III we tackle the core issue of the book—that of sensing the world around our computing devices and making sense of it.

All chapters are supported by suggested readings of the literature, and most have laboratory exercises (often involving the Phidgets sensor system). The more advanced reader is encouraged to follow the references and suggested readings in more detail, to supplement the more general discussions with additional technical detail. The course assumes some basic knowledge of programming, networks and experiment design. We do not propose to teach programming, networks or electronics in this book—there are too many good books on these topics already; however a reminder of the issues in experiment design is provided in Chap. 2.

Example Course Outline

To follow the whole book in all it's detail would make for quite a substantial course, but of course selections can be made. For instance:

- For a lower level course, omit most of the readings of research literature.
- Where Phidgets are not available, omit some of the more practical sections in Part III and re-work with design exercises or adapt to other tool-kits, e.g. Arduino.
- For a course which focuses less on particular issues in sensing or has less mathematically advanced students, omit or reduce the coverage of Chaps. 6 and 8.
- For a course more concerned with sensors than pervasive computing per-se, omit or reduce the coverage of chapters in Part II.

Aims, Learning Outcomes and Syllabus

The book expands around the notes developed while teaching a 3rd year and masters level course at the University of Sussex. The course had the following specification, which might be adapted in using this text do develop new courses:

The "pervasive computing" course aims to provide an understanding of the issues, technologies and concepts underlying the vision of pervasive computing, particularly in wireless networks, context-awareness, sensors and programming for limited and mobile devices. The course also provides experience of scientific and engineering techniques of design, experimentation, writing and critical review of literature. This is achieved through a combination of lectures on basic concepts and theory, seminars discussing literature and design, lab exercises in implementing systems with these technologies, and independent study building on this class work.

By the end of the course, a successful student should be able to:

- Categorise, describe and relate concepts in mobile and ad-hoc networks, context awareness, and programming of devices in pervasive computing environments—and make a critical review of work in the research literature which engages those concepts.
- Analyse theories and existing solutions, and design implementations and extensions to these, to solve problems in mobile and ad-hoc networks; context awareness; and programming of devices in pervasive computing environments.
- Undertake the design, running and reporting of experiments with sensors and mobile devices.make

  Outline syllabus:

- Research and practise in context awareness

- – Interfacing to sensors
- – Classification of context and uses of context
- – Resource discovery and system configuration
- – Location aware computing—sensing, modelling, representing and using location information
- Concepts in mobile and ad-hoc networks
  - – Principles in wireless communications
  - – Addressing and routing in the mobile Internet
  - – Identity and routing in ad-hoc networks
  - – Identity, routing and in-network processing in sensor networks
- Design of pervasive computing systems
  - – Programming with memory, CPU and power limitations for mobile devices and sensors
  - – Responding to context and resources: exceptions, errors and recovery
- Design and reporting of experiments
  - – Examining the literature related to the above
  - – Research and engineering questions
  - – Running experiments and reporting results

Brighton, UK   Dan Chalmers

Acknowledgements

There are many who have helped or encouraged me along the way. I will not try to list everyone, for fear of offending by omission. However, there are a few people whose influence cannot go unmentioned:

Professor Morris Sloman and Dr. Naranker Dulay, at Imperial College London, for supervising my MSc, PhD and post-doc research, which is a significant influence on this book, and generally letting me find out that I enjoy research and teaching.

Dr Ian Wakeman, Dr Des Watson and Dr Ian Mackie, amongst many at Sussex, for their support, advice and encouraging me to write this.

My doctoral students, whose problems have inspired several sections. My undergraduate students who have given feedback and been enthused enough by drafts of this to turn it into a book.

Many people at Springer, for a lot of patience when things didn't go to plan.

Sarah and my girls, for giving me the time and support to write this.

Contents

7   Sources, Models and Use of Location: *A Special Sort of Context* . . . 109
  7.1   Uses of Location 109
  7.2   Coordinate Models 111
        7.2.1   GIS 111
        7.2.2   Points of Reference 112
        7.2.3   Conversion Between Coordinate Models 114
        7.2.4   Human Descriptions 114
        7.2.5   Relationships 115
        7.2.6   Summary 116
  7.3   Sources of Location Data 117
        7.3.1   Cellular Systems 118
        7.3.2   Multi-Reference Point Systems 119
        7.3.3   Tagging 122
        7.3.4   Fingerprints and Scenes 125
        7.3.5   Summary 126
  7.4   Storing and Searching Location Data 128
        7.4.1   R-Trees 128
        7.4.2   Spatial Relations 129
  7.5   Summary 131
  7.6   Suggested Readings 132
  7.7   Laboratory Exercises: Process and Store Location Data 133
  7.8   Laboratory Exercises: Beacons and Location 134
  7.9   Laboratory Exercises: Smart-Phone Location 135
        References 136

8   Time Dependent Data 137
  8.1   Context in Time 137
        8.1.1   State Based Systems 137
        8.1.2   Event Based Systems 140
  8.2   Frequency Domain Models 140
        8.2.1   Magnitude 141
        8.2.2   Zero Crossing 142
        8.2.3   Fourier Transforms 142
  8.3   Prediction 145
        8.3.1   Recent Trends 145
        8.3.2   Interpolation and Related Sensors 146
        8.3.3   Long-Term History 146
        8.3.4   Learning 147
  8.4   Summary 147
  8.5   Suggested Readings 148
  8.6   Laboratory Exercises: Motion Sensors 148
  8.7   Laboratory Exercises: People Detection in a Large Space 148
  8.8   Laboratory Exercises: Accelerometers 149
  8.9   Laboratory Exercises: Sound 150
        References 150

List of Figures

List of Tables

List of Tables

List of Listings

Part I
Introduction

Chapter 1
Introduction:
The Computer for the 21st Century

1.1 What Is Pervasive Computing?

Pervasive computing as a field of research identifies its basis in an article by Mark Weiser of Xerox PARC [31] in 1991, and a second related paper in 1993 [32], arising from work starting in 1988. The vision is summarised well in Weiser's words:

> The most profound technologies are those that disappear. They weave themselves into the fabric of everyday life until they are indistinguishable from it. ... We are therefore trying to conceive a new way of thinking about computers, one that takes into account the human world and allows the computers themselves to vanish into the background.

At the time Weiser described his vision many of the technologies were anticipated rather than in-place, but wireless networking, processors, miniaturisation, displays, batteries etc. have all moved on since then, so that many of the technical barriers are no longer so significant—see [30] for a review of progress to 2002. We shall not build obsolescence into this text by describing the current state of the art, but we return to these issues which constrain and define pervasive computing in Sect. 1.3.

The idea of computers disappearing has led to a great emphasis on physical size. Certainly, for some applications, very small size is an advantage—however this was not the key point. To make computing blend into the environment requires that they are just part of life, having a form factor that is easy to use, not demanding attention other than that required for the desired function. At the same time computers need to do more than tools such as hammers or pen and paper, so making them usable without distracting from the task at hand requires greater sophistication. Key to this sophistication is an awareness of the *context of use* and the ability to *communicate* between devices.

While the vision emerged as recently as 1991, the roots go back further—into research on wireless networks, distributed systems, mobile computing, user interfaces, home automation, robotics, system architectures and so on. In some ways the excitement is that this vision brings together many computer science problems, and requires that they tackle much greater requirements of scale and variation. Various papers describe the challenges that are presented, including [1, 15, 16, 20, 26, 32].

D. Chalmers, *Sensing and Systems in Pervasive Computing*,
Undergraduate Topics in Computer Science,
DOI 10.1007/978-0-85729-841-6_1, © Springer-Verlag London Limited 2011

In the UK this has recently been crystallised in a "Grand Challenge in Ubiquitous Computing" [11].

Pervasive computing is also known (with varying and subtle distinctions) as "Ubiquitous Computing" (Weiser's original term, although he also used the word "pervasive"), "The Disappearing Computer" and "Ambient Computing"; while "Mobile Computing" and "Sensor Networks" can be treated as significantly overlapping fields. For our purposes we are concentrating on some systems aspects of what we shall call "Pervasive Computing". In particular we shall concern ourselves with sensing and interfacing to the world outside the computer, particularly to support context awareness; to support this interest we shall also discuss experimental practise, hardware, networking (in particular sensor networks), systems software, programming and resource management. We shall leave out much: the human interface deserves at least one book / course of its own; many finer points and new results shall be omitted to try and convey the core, established concepts. However, we are hoping that we will convey ideas and build skills in research which can be applied to further study—taking the topics we address further or exploring the wider field.

1.2 Some Classic Pervasive Computing Applications

At this stage it is helpful to consider how this technology might be used. We shall introduce a few "classic" pervasive computing applications, whose ideas and problems will thread their way through the later chapters.

1.2.1 Tourist Guide

Many researchers have produced some form of tourist guide, often based around a single location, e.g. [2, 6, 14]. These are characterised by a need for location based services: forming tours, assisting in navigation, and presentation of information relevant to the attraction or display that the user is currently seeing, i.e. an electronic tour guide. The provision of these services will typically require wireless networking as well as location detection. At the same time there are issues of usability: the device must be portable, easy to use despite being hand-held and under varying lighting conditions. Also it is desirable that the device presents interesting and useful information: so tailoring tours to the age, interests, available time and native language of the users.

Beyond the basic role as route planner and guide book the application may provide other, more interactive, benefits [2]: Recording the visit and annotating that recording with relevant information, to allow the experience to be replayed with more interaction than a (video) camera provides, or to follow up a visit with further reading; to identify exhibits which are hard to label, such as animals or distant objects, by appearance; to give multi-lingual information and act as translator / phrase

book to assist face-to-face interaction; to obtain reservations, give advice on opening times and special events, avoid crowds and traffic jams, and other time-sensitive
information.

1.2.2 Smart Office

Smart offices, or indeed smart spaces more generally, have been a broad theme for
much pervasive computing research. Most researchers have an office space which
can double up as a laboratory, and many shared and personal devices are in use. The
technologies and issues for smart spaces in general are discussed at length in [12].
The typical smart office application combines location awareness with systems for
display of information, interaction or messaging.

A good early example of this research theme is the active badge system [29],
developed at Olivetti, later AT&T, research labs in Cambridge, UK. It provided a
system of badges, to be worn or attached to objects of interest, and sensors embedded in the building to locate these badges. This enabled applications based on
locating people or objects, such as routing of phone calls, relocation of computing
desktops [19], identification of who is in the building etc. The original badges used
infra-red communications, but these were later developed using ultrasonics [19]. As
much as the design is interesting, these systems quickly reveal complex issues in
deployment and user perception [18].

1.2.3 Sensing the Natural Environment

There have been several projects where sensor networks have been used to monitor
the natural world, including sea-birds [22], forests [28] and glaciers [23]. These
applications are typified by inaccessibility, requiring maintenance (and so power
consumption) to be minimised; a demanding environment for packaging; a need to
be unobtrusive; to have a wireless network which is robust in the face of difficult
deployment, device failure and device movement; and a need to report appropriately
on what has been sensed to a distant base. We shall see later that there are trade-offs
here, particularly between what is sensed and how it is reported.

1.2.4 Games

Games which exploit sensors and take place in the wider world using sensors are
becoming commonplace and used as a vehicle by many researchers [8]. The Nin-
tendo Wii allows the user to use gesture and be unplugged from the console, but
still restricts the user to a limited space. Modern mobile phone platforms, such as

the iOS/iPhone and Android/smart phone, containing GPS and accelerometers allow gesture, location and communication to be used in new ways. Games involving GPS such as [7] exploit the nature of sensors and take place over wider areas [21]. Other recreational, sporting and artistic activities, such as using mobile phones to exchange personal information [3, 4], geocaching[1], adding to open source mapping[2], creating located media e.g.[3,4], locative art [17] use sensor technologies, an interplay with the world around them and communications to form their basis in various ways.

1.2.5 Everyday Objects

Many pervasive computing prototypes that you will find in the literature are playful experiments with ideas, rather than polished products—they are designed to explore what is possible and how people react to them. Making everyday objects, such as picture frames, cups, fridges etc. intelligent has provided many insights. Sometimes the goal is to simplify and automate routine activities, but often it is simply to explore a richer more connected environment.

The "mediacups" project at TecO [5] is a good example of this, in which coffee cups had sensors, processing and networking capability built into them. It is pervasive, in that the cups are not presenting themselves as computers. It goes beyond *embedded computing* in that the design expects ad-hoc information sharing between cups and similarly enhanced objects, and as the cups will sense and respond to their environment.

An example of using sensors to simplify fiddly routine activities is given in [24].

In this devices are shaken together to provide authentication, rather than manually setting up keys. Accelerometer readings are taken, patterns extracted and compared: if the shaking of two devices is sufficiently similar then the devices are considered to be authenticated to each other. It would be hard for an intruder to arrange for their device to share exactly the same pattern of acceleration and also gain the same key.

1.2.6 Mobile Phones

Mobile phones are arguably a device rather than an application, but here they represent mobile information access and messaging. They are hugely successful and

---

[1]http://www.geocaching.com/.

[2]http://www.openstreetmap.org/.

[3]http://www.locative-media.org/.

[4]http://www.geograph.org.uk/.

popular, and network coverage is widespread even in remote areas—so they can be considered pervasive. However, they remain interesting because they still present limitations in their battery life, processing power and user interfaces; the experience of inappropriate ringing suggests better awareness of social situations would be an advantage; their association with other devices (blue-tooth headsets, PCs for address book management etc.) is a good example of personal area networking; and their use as interfaces to other applications, e.g. micro-blogging and information sharing [3], makes them an interesting and widely used platform.

1.3 What Are the Research Problems in Pervasive Computing?

Right from the beginning a wide range of computer science problems were associated with pervasive computing [32]. In some cases these were extensions of existing problems relating to distributed systems, mobility and hardware [26] (and some of the issues of limited systems resurrect problems that technology advances have removed in the desktop). Since 1991 technology has moved on: and to some extent this was expected and contributed to the idea of pervasive computing, and can continue to be expected and contribute to new ideas we think of today. However, there are some basic problems which make pervasive computing hard and interesting. Many of these come down to *people, power, scale* and *variation* (which we expand on below); but are manifested in many issues, including: size, energy, processing, memory, communications, architecture, deployment, management, interfaces, context sensing, security etc. We can also think of these problems as topics within fields of computer science research: formal theories to represent and reason about systems which *must* work well; human interaction as it affects individuals and societies; systems engineering; programming languages and the design of software; and the description and representation of ideas and content to communicate. This book is aimed at undergraduate and post-graduate students, which implies that we now have some well-formed ideas and technologies in the area; however, this does not mean that each one is ideal nor that the combination solves all the issues—this is still (in 2010) a busy and interesting research field. It is hoped that we may inspire some of our readers to push the field on still further, or apply these ideas to similar problems in other fields.

1.3.1 People

We are concentrating on systems issues here, but often example applications are used to verify our ideas, and the systems we design cannot exclude interaction with people in their design. Interfaces are required to form the connection between people and computing an a pervasive environment. The interface must provide utility, but can be subtle and should aim for natural simplicity, but this is an unpredictable and human domain, which does not easily submit to simple rules. Communication makes these things interesting—an interaction with a person may generate many systems interactions to achieve a goal. Many systems also use natural networks, formed by proximity of users, motion of people or social networks and trust relationships between users, e.g. [25].

There are also environmental concerns for users: hundreds of devices which beep or flash LEDs or create heat will be obtrusive outside a server room, but these devices must be capable of reporting problems and supporting debugging, and CPU power inevitably means generating heat, so we must moderate our expectations of computing power.

1.3.2 Energy

Limited energy sources drive many decisions in pervasive computing design, in software as well as hardware. We introduce ideas here and expand on them in 3. Some devices may have the luxury of mains electricity, but this is not a routine assumption. Many of the devices being considered will be battery powered, where changing or re-charging batteries requires human intervention, which is unrealistic on any great scale. Adding to the battery changing burden is unlikely to help and devices are not mobile while plugged in for charging. There are also environmental concerns: replacing batteries in hundreds of new devices (for each of us) would not only be time consuming but environmentally disastrous, so practical re-charging strategies and ways to increase battery lifetime must be sought. Renewable sources, including solar and from motion such as walking, can help (particularly for charging) but for devices on shelves, in cupboards and in bags none of these is a universal energy source. Typically, the solution is to reduce power use so that battery changing is acceptably infrequent, or so devices last between charging opportunities, or simply last long enough and are then discarded.

In ICs power consumption is generally proportional to the square of the supply voltage and linear with clock speed (lower supply voltage forces slower speed in many circuits) and the number of bits being switched. The use of pipelines can reduce the impact of slower clock speeds. Larger circuits can have lower power consumption for a given speed, at the expense of feature count.

Reducing the number of bits is not a problem for many applications, but it does affect the ease of representing large numbers and of addressing large memories. Many sensor network devices use 8-bit micro-controllers running at clock speeds of a few MHz (e.g. Atmel ATMega, Microchip PIC and various 8051 variants) to reduce the power consumption and chip count. Imported libraries and tools (e.g. Java) which do not consider 8-bit use in their design can result in complex code and inefficient use of memory for the problem. Good algorithm selection and compiler optimisation are therefore important, saving energy also implies saving computing power.

The principle of efficient design is particularly important in communications protocol design. Transmission, reception and listening on a wireless link all have a significant power cost. Protocol design should therefore seek to minimise headers, compress data, avoid re-transmission and avoid having the radio on to listen when no communications are expected.

Switching things off is a technique which can be applied beyond the network, to the CPU (where selection of a device with sleep modes and slow modes is helpful) and to peripherals and circuits which are only used occasionally (where devices can be switched on when needed).

1.3.3 Scale

Miniaturisation of components continues: the computing power that used to fill a large room is now contained in a desktop box; the computing power that used to fill a desktop box now fits in a mobile phone, and so on. Certainly, for some applications, very small size is an advantage—however pervasive computing is about much more than making computers disappear because we have made them too small to notice. Pervasive computing expects a quantity and density of devices that makes the Internet look small-scale—imagine computers that are deployed like paint, at the extreme. This large scale brings great complexity, although individual devices can become simpler and more specialised.

Communications become more complex in several ways. Firstly, consider approaches to medium access. If these very small devices use ad-hoc arrangements of broadcast networks then controlling competition for bandwidth could lead to very long delays to access the network, very low bandwidth, or very localised communication requiring many routing hops. Addressing and routing complexity also becomes much more complex in a pervasive computing environment. Many personal and organisational networks will overlap and move through the environment. Managing identifiers in a scalable way becomes harder as location and ownership/authority are constantly changing. Managing routing in an efficient way becomes harder as with many more nodes, whose relationships change rapidly, identifying good routes is hard.

Decentralisation and multiple overlapping management domains also makes management of devices hard. Consider the problem of keeping software up to date in a network of PCs, some on, others off; some laptops, some servers; some where the user has administration rights etc. Increasing the number and diversity of devices doesn't simplify this, and is compounded by problems in determining who has what rights to a given device—particularly if some rights have been delegated in order to gain other privileges.

1.3.4 Variation

Last, but not least, is the problem of variation. The large scale and limitations of pervasive computing are not a static situation. There will be a range of devices of different capabilities, just as Weiser expected a range of devices with different form factors. There will be a variety of networks, a variety of location systems, a variety of sensors etc. The devices, and networks they form, will move around the world, attached to people, vehicles, animals, furniture. Again, there is variation across several scales, here in time and distance: people move about all the time with weekday and weekend patterns, furniture moves rather more occasionally with houses and offices. Other variations in use of the environment, available power, and expected behaviour will occur with seasons, school terms, growing up and growing old etc. So, if we are to build pervasive computing into homes and buildings we must expect it to be adaptable, to be added to, to be used in different ways—in exactly the same way as good buildings are adaptable [9].

A key consideration in dealing with variation is what the user is protected from and what the user is exposed to. A well established principle in distributed systems is transparency, where the higher levels do not need to be aware of whether a service is local or remote, e.g. networked file systems. In a highly variable environment however this must break down at some point, and where the user is changing their location, social context etc. the user cannot help but be aware of changes in the environment [21]. Where a pervasive computing system adapts to the current environment the challenge then becomes to make changes in behaviour explicable in relation to the user's experience. This requires accurate and timely interpretation of sensor data. When accurate becomes hard to achieve then graceful degradation should end in user involvement.

As discussed above, networks will be subject to great variation. There are large scale variations, as devices move between networks: in the access encoding, in the bandwidth available, in the ownership and rights to use allowed. Within a network there are also small-scale variations, due to other devices' usage and environmental conditions. To manage these variations systems need to adapt to the current conditions, making reasonable use of the network to gain acceptable performance. In some situations resources will need to be reserved or migrated; work performed speculatively or delayed until resources are available; or interactions adapted, as appropriate to the network characteristics [10].

Devices also cause variation for software which must be widely deployable or mobile at run-time. The CPU power, memory, network bandwidth, and network range of small devices may all improve but will continue to lag behind "traditional" computing; battery (and other power) technology will improve but will remain limited in comparison to mains electricity. Devices deployed in the environment will have varying capacities, long lifetimes, be complex to micro-administer and connect to devices outside the owner's control, so systems must expect great variety in the devices that form them.

In summary, variation—across devices, locations of use and time will require detection and appropriate adaptation. The massive scale of deployment will require new approaches to make algorithms and resources scale with the demands of this complexity. Power, in computing terms and energy terms, will be scarce requiring care in the design of algorithms and systems will add to these concerns for design and resource management. Finally, the need for users to find these systems natural to use and beneficial must be remembered in their design—and the user's part in identifying and responding to changes in the system and its environment should not be underestimated, even focusing on systems issues as we shall here. In all these issues we should look for good solutions to the engineering problems; look for underlying theories and models which can be applied; and look for imaginative designs for the user's experience whose greatest success will be to disappear from the user's attention.

1.4   Outline of the Book

The discussion above of the nature of pervasive computing and the broad issues that it raises is simply an introduction. In the following chapters we shall discuss some of these problems in rather more depth and examine solutions that have been found and look for common techniques to be applied in this domain.

This text is intended for final year (3rd or 4th year in the UK) undergraduate and masters students studying systems led courses in pervasive computing or advanced topics in networking; it should also be useful to doctoral students tackling pervasive computing for the first time and might form part of a course for undergraduate engineering students. Each chapter is designed to be accompanied by wider reading, ideally to be discussed in a seminar class; and also by lab work; lectures can be used to present and build on the grounding material presented here. The readings are designed to encourage deeper study of the subject and flexibility to pursue personal interests; they are also intended to support a well-founded, scientific approach to ideas, experiments and writing. The lab work is designed to explore the real problems behind the ideas presented and also to encourage a scientific approach to design, performance and reporting of experiments.

Part II expands on some of the challenges of pervasive computing described above and surveys some of the tools which are already well established. In this we look at hardware: computing platforms and sensors; networks: including Bluetooth, ZigBee, 802.11, mobile IP and system software.

Part III deals with the issues of sensing the world outside the computer, capturing the variations that pervasive computing will expose users to. We examine the idea of context, and look particularly closely at location, and also sensing of the environment. We also consider the problems of error that are inevitable in sensing and reasoning about the view of the world formed. For this part of the book, the labs are based around the Phidgets toolkit[5]. This is a pragmatic choice: They are affordibly priced; their USB interface to PCs lowers the start-up barrier to use; code executing on the PC simplifies debugging, and libraries and APIs are available for several popular languages. While enjoying the ease of use, it should be remembered that using sensors on an 8-bit battery powered platform will present additional challenges, which is a recurring theme. Other tool-kits may be used if they are already

---

[5]http://www.phidgets.com/.

available, the lab work assumes a reasonable level of (Java) programming skill and so concentrates on guiding experiments rather than providing detailed recipes.

1.5 Suggested Readings

1.5.1 General Readings

- Weiser's visions of pervasive computing
  - Mark Weiser. The computer for the 21st century. *Scientific American*, 3:94–104, September 1991
  - Mark Weiser. Some computer science issues in ubiquitous computing. *Communications of the ACM*, 36(7):75–84, 1993
- Discussions of research issues and challenges
  - Nigel Davies and Hans-Werner Gellersen. Beyond prototypes: Challenges in deploying ubiquitous systems. *IEEE Pervasive Computing*, 1(1):26–35, 2002
  - Gregory D. Abowd and Elizabeth D. Mynatt. Charting past, present, and future research in ubiquitous computing. *ACM Transactions on Computer-Human Interaction*, 7(1):29–58, 2000
  - Mahadev Satyanarayanan. Pervasive computing: Vision and challenges. *IEEE Personal Communications*, 8(4):10–17, 2001

1.5.2 Readings on Exemplar Applications

- Tourist guides:
  - Gregory D. Abowd, Christopher G. Atkeson, Jason I. Hong, Sue Long, Rob Kooper, and Mike Pinkerton. Cyberguide: A mobile context-aware tour guide. *Wireless Networks*, 3(5):421–433, 1997
  - Nigel Davies, Keith Cheverst, Keith Mitchell, and Alon Efrat. Using and determining location in a context-sensitive tour guide. *IEEE Computer*, 34(8):35–41, 2001
- Sensing the natural environment:
  - Robert Szewczyk, Eric Osterweil, Joseph Polastre, Michael Hamilton, Alan M. Mainwaring, and Deborah Estrin. Habitat monitoring with sensor networks. *Communications of the ACM*, 47(6):34–40, 2004
- Smart offices:
  - Diane J. Cook and Sajal K. Das, editors. *Smart Environments*. Wiley, 2005
  - Andy Harter, Andy Hopper, Pete Steggles, Andy Ward, and Paul Webster. The anatomy of a context-aware application. *Wireless Networks*, 8(2–3):187–197, 2002

- Games:
  - Arianna Bassoli, Johanna Brewer, Karen Martin, Paul Dourish, and Scott Mainwaring. Underground aesthetics: Rethinking urban computing. *IEEE Pervasive Computing*, 6(3):39–45, 2007
  - Steve Benford, Andy Crabtree, Martin Flintham, Adam Drozd, Rob Anastasi, Mark Paxton, Nick Tandavanitj, Matt Adams, and Ju Row-Farr. Can you see me now? *ACM Trans. Comput.-Hum. Interact.*, 13(1):100–133, 2006
- Everyday objects:
  - Michael Beigl, Hans-Werner Gellersen, and Albrecht Schmidt. Mediacups: experience with design and use of computer-augmented everyday artefacts. *Computer Networks*, 35(4):401–409, 2001

1.6 Laboratory Exercises: Getting Started with Phidgets

The purpose of this lab is to become familiar with using Phidgets and their API.

1. Connect the main Phidget board to the USB port. If there is a readily-available toolkit available for your platform, confirm that it is correctly detected.
2. Connect a rotation sensor (potentiometer voltage divider) to one of the analogue ports. Write a small program to report the value read. To do this find the Phidgets jar file and explore the API documentation a little:
   com.phidgets.InterfaceKitPhidget is a good place to start. Consider any options (polling, event listening and more specialised classes) that might be appropriate.
3. Connect a multi-coloured LED board to the digital outputs. Take care to correctly connect the ground line and driving lines the right way round. Use the API/toolkit to test the connection.

   If you are building your own LED board, be aware that the Phidget interface kit has built in resistors, so many LEDs can be driven with no further circuitry. We have used the parts as shown in Table 1.1, available from CPC/Farnell, but there are many alternatives.
4. Use the rotation sensor to select different coloured LEDs. Select a range of values to activate each LED, and change the digital outputs when the analogue input moves between ranges. Consider whether state-polling or event driven behaviours are most appropriate here. Consider appropriate behaviour when ranges overlap.
5. Experiment with driving multiple LEDs in a traffic light pattern. Use history (previous state and/or previous reading) to detect direction of change in sensor to the create red–red & yellow–green–yellow–red cycle. You might also want to experiment with timers to ensure that transient input values are ignored, or traffic lights change at a sensible rate, particularly if your Java threads programming is rusty.
6. Explore the properties of light sensors and LEDs. Use a light sensor to measure the light level from an LED. Take multiple readings and see what average and

Table 1.1 LED indicator parts

Mfr.	Part no.	Colour (nm)	Power (mW)	Intensity (mcd)	View (°)
CML	CMD57124A	635 (R)	120	6	100
CML	CMD53124A	585 (Y)	120	6	100
CML	CMD54124A	562 (G)	120	6	100
Toshiba	TLGE159P(F)	574 (G)	140	1400	20

standard deviation you experience—and then put the sensors in a dark environment (taping a box over the work-bench will probably suffice) and see whether you get more repeatable results. Finally, vary the angle of the LED to the sensor and at which the light hits the sensor—does this affect the readings? The lab 5.8 builds on the ideas here, but this gives a taste of the issues you will tackle there.

References

1. Abowd, G.D., Mynatt, E.D.: Charting past, present, and future research in ubiquitous computing. ACM Trans. Comput.-Hum. Interact. **7**(1), 29–58 (2000)
2. Abowd, G.D., Atkeson, C.G., Hong, J.I., Long, S., Kooper, R., Pinkerton, M.: Cyberguide: a mobile context-aware tour guide. Wirel. Netw. **3**(5), 421–433 (1997)
3. Bassoli, A., Brewer, J., Martin, K., Dourish, P., Mainwaring, S.: Underground aesthetics: rethinking urban computing. IEEE Pervasive Comput. **6**(3), 39–45 (2007)
4. Baumann, S., Jung, B., Bassoli, A., Wisniowski, M.: Bluetuna: let your neighbour know what music you like. In: CHI '07: CHI '07 Extended Abstracts on Human Factors in Computing Systems, pp. 1941–1946. ACM, New York (2007)
5. Beigl, M., Gellersen, H.-W., Schmidt, A.: Mediacups: experience with design and use of computer-augmented everyday artefacts. Comput. Netw. **35**(4), 401–409 (2001)
6. Bellotti, F., Berta, R., De Gloria, A., Margarone, M.: IEEE pervasive computing: integrated environments—user testing a hypermedia tour guide. IEEE Distrib. Syst. Online **3**(6) (2002)
7. Benford, S., Crabtree, A., Flintham, M., Drozd, A., Anastasi, R., Paxton, M., Tandavanitj, N., Adams, M., Row-Far, J.: Can you see me now? ACM Trans. Comput.-Hum. Interact. **13**(1), 100–133 (2006)
8. Björk, S., Holopainen, J., Ljungstrand, P., Mandryk, R.: Special issue on ubiquitous games. Pers. Ubiquitous Comput. **6**(5–6), 358–361 (2002)
9. Brand, S.: How Buildings Learn: What Happens After They're Built. Viking Press, New York (1994)
10. Chalmers, D., Sloman, M.: A survey of quality of service in mobile computing environments. IEEE Commun. Surv. **2**, 2–10 (1999)
11. Chalmers, D., Chalmers, M., Crowcroft, J., Kwiatkowska, M., Milner, R., O'Neill, E., Rodden, T., Sassone, V., Sloman, M.: Ubiquitous computing: experience, design and science. Technical report, UKCRC Grand Challenge in Ubiquitous Computing Committee (2006)
12. Cook, D.J., Das, S.K. (eds.): Smart Environments. Wiley, New York (2005)
13. Davies, N., Gellersen, H.-W.: Beyond prototypes: challenges in deploying ubiquitous systems. IEEE Pervasive Comput. **1**(1), 26–35 (2002)
14. Davies, N., Cheverst, K., Mitchell, K., Efrat, A.: Using and determining location in a context-sensitive tour guide. IEEE Comput. **34**(8), 35–41 (2001)
15. Duchamp, D.: Issues in wireless mobile computing. In: 3rd IEEE Workshop on Workstation Operating Systems (1992)

16. Forman, G.H., Zahorjan, J.: The challenges of mobile computing. IEEE Comput. **27**(4), 38–47 (1994)
17. Gibson, W.: Spook Country. Penguin, Baltimore (2007)
18. Harle, R.K., Hopper, A.: Deploying and evaluating a location-aware system. In: Shin, K.G., Kotz, D., Noble, B.D. (eds.) MobiSys, pp. 219–232. ACM, New York (2005)
19. Harter, A., Hopper, A., Steggles, P., Ward, A., Webster, P.: The anatomy of a context-aware application. Wirel. Netw. **8**(2–3), 187–197 (2002)
20. Imielinski, T., Badrinath, B.R.: Mobile wireless computing: challenges in data management. Commun. ACM **37**(10), 18–28 (1994)
21. MacColl, I., Chalmers, M., Rogers, Y., Smith, H.: Seamful ubiquity: beyond seamless integration. In: Proc. Ubicomp 2002 Workshop on Models and Concepts for Ubiquitous Computing (2002)
22. Mainwaring, A.M., Culler, D.E., Polastre, J., Szewczyk, R., Anderson, J.: Wireless sensor networks for habitat monitoring. In: Raghavendra, C.S., Sivalingam, K.M. (eds.) WSNA, pp. 88–97. ACM, New York (2002)
23. Martinez, K., Hart, J.K., Ong, R.: Environmental sensor networks. IEEE Comput. **37**(8), 50–56 (2004)
24. Mayrhofer, R., Gellersen, H.: Shake well before use: authentication based on accelerometer data. In: LaMarca, A., Langheinrich, M., Truong, K.N. (eds.) Pervasive. Lecture Notes in Computer Science, vol. 4480, pp. 144–161. Springer, Berlin (2007)
25. McNamara, L., Mascolo, C., Capra, L.: Media sharing based on colocation prediction in urban transport. In: MobiCom '08: Proceedings of the 14th ACM International Conference on Mobile Computing and Networking, pp. 58–69. ACM, New York (2008)
26. Satyanarayanan, M.: Pervasive computing: vision and challenges. IEEE Pers. Commun. **8**(4), 10–17 (2001)
27. Szewczyk, R., Osterweil, E., Polastre, J., Hamilton, M., Mainwaring, A.M., Estrin, D.: Habitat monitoring with sensor networks. Commun. ACM **47**(6), 34–40 (2004)
28. Tolle, G., Polastre, J., Szewczyk, R., Culler, D.E., Turner, N., Tu, K., Burgess, S., Dawson, T., Buonadonna, P., Gay, D., Hong, W.: A macroscope in the redwoods. In: Redi, J., Balakrishnan, H., Zhao, F. (eds.) SenSys, pp. 51–63. ACM, New York (2005)
29. Want, R., Hopper, A., Falcao, V., Gibbons, J.: The active badge location system. ACM Trans. Inf. Syst. **10**(1), 91–102 (1992)
30. Want, R., Borriello, G., Pering, T., Farkas, K.I.: Disappearing hardware. IEEE Pervasive Comput. **01**(1), 36–47 (2002)
31. Weiser, M.: The computer for the 21st century. Sci. Am. **3**, 94–104 (1991)
32. Weiser, M.: Some computer science issues in ubiquitous computing. Commun. ACM **36**(7), 75–84 (1993)

Chapter 2
Pointers on Experiments and Results

This chapter is designed as a refresher on the issues of experiment design and presentation of results. We shall not be presenting an exhaustive survey nor treating the issues in great depth as there are many books which address the points in this chapter already, e.g. [1], although a traditional maths and science secondary school education or science degree ought to cover most of the issues and any university library will have a selection of research methods texts.

2.1 Hypothesis

In science it would be common to start an experiment by defining a hypothesis. This is a "proposition made as a basis for reasoning, without the assumption of its truth; a supposition made as a starting point for further investigation from known facts; a groundless assumption" [4]. The explanation is *proposed* because it does not fit existing models or theories—it may add to them, modify them or replace them. This requires that we have both observed some phenomenon which requires explaining or allows us to make a prediction; and have an explanation that we can test. For some cases the hypothesis will be tested statistically, in others to be true or false. A variation on this is the "null hypothesis", that there is no difference between a sample and either the whole population or some other population according to a measure—a proposition that this measure is not significant in the definition of the test sample.

Of course rather than the "science" approach, we might adopt the research methods of other disciplines. In particular, ethnography is widely used in pervasive computing—where studies are geared to understanding what people do with the world around them, in a natural (or at least naturalistic) setting. This approach is most commonly used in HCI focused research, which isn't the focus of this book. However, those expecting to continue with research in this area should be aware of a variety of methods and the other methods that they might encounter. The following may be interesting reading in this area: [2].

D. Chalmers, *Sensing and Systems in Pervasive Computing*,
Undergraduate Topics in Computer Science,
DOI 10.1007/978-0-85729-841-6_2, © Springer-Verlag London Limited 2011

We might also try to define a "research question"—wondering "what happens if
…". This might be "what happens if we give people this system to use" (prompting
ethnography) or "what happens if we apply certain stimulus to a system", typically
one which is too complex or whose workings are too opaque for us to make a prediction. As we form a better model of how this class of systems are used, or how
the system behaves under a class of stimuli we may move from this open ended
approach (which done badly is poking about in the dark and done well is blue sky
thinking) towards a traditional hypothesis.

Finally, we may set ourselves an engineering problem and define a set of constraints and evaluate whether a system meets them, or which system meets them at
least cost. In such an approach we need to beware of setting arbitrary targets. Existing infrastructure may set constraints and existing competition may set targets, but
with research which is further away from deployment it becomes easier to argue for
revisions in these constraints.

A question or hypothesis in computer systems is often framed in terms of a comparison, e.g. "system X is better than system Y". The systems under comparison
may take various forms:

- Some existing system, which we believe a different approach can better.
- A single system running with different parameters. Parameters may be tuning
  variables, number of nodes in a network, deployment hardware, workload data
  etc.
- Well known base cases, typified by either an exhaustive algorithm, a random algorithm or a theoretical best case. The first two are often encountered in networking literature while the latter is found when evaluating algorithms that use some
  heuristic or approximation to gain a cost advantage.

A null-hypothesis would suggest that two systems are effectively identical under a
given measure, despite whatever difference has been created.

2.1.1 Measures and Conditions

Occasionally it is sufficient to say that an algorithm "works" or meets some criteria,
or provide observations of the use of a system, but more often we want to answer
some combination of questions, such as:

- Is system x or y better under a certain range of conditions, on average and in the
  worst case?
- Do algorithms x, y and z scale?
- If we make a change to the configuration of x does this provide an improvement
  in speed, memory and network use over a range of work-loads?
- In what situations is x better than y?

In each case we need to make *measured* comparisons between systems with equivalent conditions. We use the plural as we generally find that we must consider both

costs and benefits, and claim superiority with a caveat. A measure will typically be numeric, with units. Care must be taken that any noise in the reading is allowed for and that sufficient samples are taken that the result is not due to chance, start-up effects or some external factor. Many experiments need repeating to gain statistical measures of performance, in which case either the conditions must be repeatable or any variation in conditions must be subject to a null hypothesis. Repeatable conditions may require stored rather than live data, e.g. from sensors, or fixed seeds in random number generation for probabilistic simulations.

The necessary dual to measures are conditions. These are the variables that can be controlled in the study—choice of algorithms, parameters for configuration, choice of data sets etc. In some cases conditions have many components, such as hardware, operating systems, other system load, environment, identity of participants etc. Note the system configuration in your experiments as all kinds of parameters might be useful for those that follow to understand how their results and yours are related and might be repeated and in later analysis some aspect may turn out to be more important than you anticipated.

Examples of measures and controls we might consider in this book include:

- CPU and memory use measured for different benchmark algorithms and workloads as controls
- network throughput measured with different packet sizes and loss rates as controls
- distribution of difference (measure, second order) between reported (measured) and actual (controlled) values from signal processing of a given data set (controlled) with different algorithms (another control)

For numeric measures and conditions we might plot a graph, typically with the measures on the y axis, the condition of interest on the x axis, and multiple lines representing discrete conditions—large scale changes in parameters, different algorithms or data sets, as illustrated in Fig. 2.1. Such a graph allows us to identify how the performance of each discrete condition compares to the others. In the example we note experimental test conditions indicated with a point, connected by lines; a theoretical result plotted as a line; "condition two, value B" has no result for $x = 1, 2$ (presumably indicating it does not function under that condition); and the two test systems each have sections of the x axis condition where they are closer to the theoretical result but that "condition two, value A" rises faster as values of "condition one" get higher.

2.2 Method

There are a number of techniques which are used to test a hypothesis:

- Argument—more or less logical, preferably with citations of facts and figures. This is a good basis for setting out a position, but does not verify that the position is correct. One comes across this in the research literature in the form of position papers, which describe early work; and in research proposals, which argue that an idea merits funding.

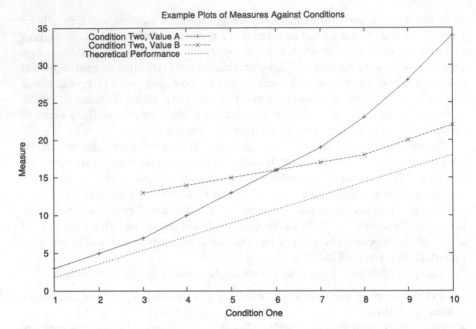

Fig. 2.1 An example plot of a measure under two conditions

- Proof—a mathematical process which shows that an idea is correct, often using logic but may use other analysis techniques. A marvellous thing, which any theoretical concept should seek. In addition one can prove properties of algorithms. However, in this text we tend to focus on applications and implementations. In these situations logic gives us confidence in an idea but relies on assumptions which need to be checked; formal techniques in programming can also be used to give confidence in an algorithm's properties and so in the smooth running of the program.
- Experiment—setting up controlled conditions and testing an implementation. This is an approach which we tend to promote in this text, as a good basis for examining the properties of sensors and of small pieces of developed code. We would urge the reader to see whether a traditional problem–hypothesis–method–results–conclusion approach to an issue is viable. If so, the approach makes the scientist readers relax and the structure tends to lead to results which are easy to analyse. However, be aware that an "experiment" in this sense usually relies on well controlled conditions and often a control case, for comparison. As a study gets closer to natural human use controlled conditions get harder to argue and complex human and external factors make results harder to analyse (requiring greater numbers of participants and more complex statistical analysis).
- Simulation, a form of experiment deserving special mention here—extracting an idealised model of the thing being studied, without the problems of live subjects in an experiment, and performing experiments on this. The models can be sophisticated enough to include some random (usually probabilistic) factors and require

multiple runs to establish average results and variations. Simulation can also be used to exhaustively test software. The limits of this approach are (rather like the mathematical proof) the accuracy of the assumptions made: would the introduction of the thing being tested change behaviour, is some issue being missed?

- Survey—watching what happens, involving techniques including questionnaires, interviews, video, observation and note-taking and instrumented software. The setting is usually as natural as possible (ideally not staged at all) while trying to minimise the involvement of the watcher for fear of altering what happens (the Hawthorne effect). The problems here are the effort required to undertake the survey and analyse the findings; the effect of the observer and the form of questions asked; the general validity of the set of subjects being observed; the problems of creating valid comparisons with different human participants—not to mention issues of funding deployment, research ethics, health and safety etc.

So, *no approach works?* Of course, each has its place and we would urge the reader to consider which is the right way of exploring the qualities of the issue under test. Often there is a progression: argument to convince peers that the idea merits consideration; then analysis to convince yourself the design is sound; then simulation to establish expected sub-system behaviour; then controlled experiment to verify correct function with real users and to review a whole-system design; then limited natural deployment to explore the subtleties that arise in prolonged use; then product for sale to make more general conclusions about a broad range of users—or some sub-set of these. In some cases our hypothesis concerns something smaller than an application or system, and simulation and experiment are the main tools, as testing algorithms and devices is usually best carried out in a physical science / engineering tradition; alternatively if the questions are more open with unanticipated outcomes then surveys and observational experiments drawing from the social sciences are more appropriate. In this text we are mostly concerned with experiments, but many of the comments which follow are applicable to experiment design through simulation and to survey design.

2.3 Collection of Data

Various data collection methods may be found in pervasive computing, including:

- Instrumenting code or log files to note system events
- Physical measurement (controlled experiment)
- Measurement of simulated system
- Timed / monitored activity, either directly, by video, by system logs etc.
- Questionnaire, interview, focus group (less applicable to testing of systems but very relevant to testing the use of systems)

Each has its own strengths and weaknesses and is applicable to different situations. None is "easy" and it is always possible to use more data—although not always possible to meet deadlines if there is more than you can process! In all cases keep your raw data and process later. It is much easier to generate new statistics and analyses from raw data in log files than it is to re-run an experiment where data is generated and processed at run-time.

If relying on instrumented code in a deployment care needs to be taken that the instrumentation tells you the values you need, with sensible units, accuracy and frequency; that any filtering and aggregation is correct. Testing of the run–data collect–data analysis cycle is time consuming. Tests in the lab may not reveal problems arising from deployment scale, timing from multiple users, environmental factors and unexpected user behaviour. Controlled experiments and simulations do not suffer from the unpredictability of "the wild" but have requirements for careful set up and data collection as above. The observation of- and interaction with- users can give vital information about *systems* research that tests on algorithms and simulators alone cannot answer. While our focus in this book has been on systems pervasive computing lends itself to applied research and the connection with users is a desirable end-point.

2.4 Analysis of Data

There are many analysis techniques and it is not our purpose to address them all. For statistical data the selection of analysis will depend on the number of variables, the type, completeness and volume of data. The results in this case will typically be presented as a correlation, with a given confidence, using a certain test over n data points—all this information is needed when reporting results. Even when reporting correct operation the range of tests and number of runs are vital pieces of information for any non-trivial system. Where sensors are involved then it is important to document the tool chain properly: what sensors, what placement, what stimulus, how many runs, processed with what algorithm, on what platform? For any experiment documenting the tools and data set is important for allowing repeatability; where interfacing with the real world is concerned proper documentation of a rigorous procedure gives confidence in the findings.

2.4.1 Presentation of Results

The results, in particular any graphs, will be read directly after the abstract by some readers. A clear message is vital to putting forward an idea, and a well presented analysis is key. Be sure to address:

- What did you find?
- How can the reader use this finding in their work?

Don't bury the message in caveats, but do make the bounds of your work clear in the method and any anomalies or unexpected findings clear in the discussion.

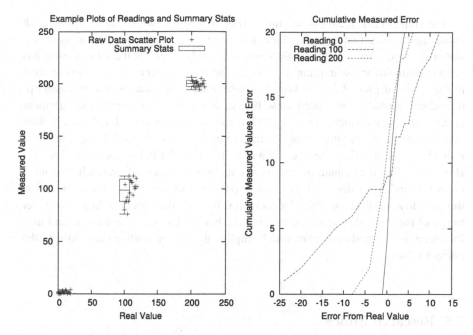

Fig. 2.2 An example of scatter and box and whisker plots for measurements of a known condition, 20 data points at each real value

So, what tools are useful? Of course this depends on the hypothesis / question / observations you made, what the form of the data and analysis is and what the findings are, but common tools include:

- Tables of data. Really only useful for simple summary data. A graph or analysis of correlation is often more useful.
- Histograms, where you have several comparisons and a few conditions to compare on one axis.
- Line graphs, where you have a small number of comparisons over a more numerous (tending to continuous) range of test points (x axis). Often the most useful form of results in considering performance of a number of alternative systems against time or controlled variables.
- Scatter plots, where something close to raw data with an accompanying discussion aids your narrative.
- Be clear about patterns of noise: is it Gaussian, long tail, something else? What have you done to mitigate it? Have you shown standard mean, mode or median, deviation, percentile, limits in e.g. box/whisker plots?
- Textual statement of statistical findings. A simple test of a hypothesis with a clear claim attached, qualified with confidence and number of data points.

Most research methods texts will expand on the presentation of data, and for a particular research area following the norms of that community is fairly safe, but for a deeper read on this Tufte's book is excellent [3].

The graph in Fig. 2.2 illustrates the plotting of raw data with a scatter graph (each value slightly offset on the x axis for clarity) and box and whisker plots of summary statistics: *min, mean − stddev, mean, mean + stddev, max*. Standard deviation has been used due to an assumption about Gaussian noise, percentiles are also common in this form of plot. It can be seen that where the real value is zero the assumption about normally distributed noise breaks down, as the minimum measurement is zero. The measurements for $x = 100$ have a much wider spread, reflected in their standard deviation and minimum and maximum bars; we also see that although the noise is essentially Gaussian there is a significant outlier below the mean. We also show a graph of the cumulative counts of data points at each difference between the measured and real value, with three lines: one for each real value. The x-axis plots the error to normalise the scales for each plot. We note that this also shows the wider range of the $x = 100$ condition, the positive bias of the $x = 0$ condition, and also the steep rise around zero error which implies that many readings are close to the correct value.

2.5 Research Ethics

Last, but by no means least—when designing experiments which sense human activity and are deployed into the world ethics and safety must be considered. Most research organisations will have a research ethics process, where someone independent will ask questions of research involving people, e.g.:

- Is it physically safe? What has been done to manage any risks, e.g. selection of participants, adjustments to the method, provision of assistance and emergency procedures.
- Might people be upset? What has been done to avoid this and/or handle it when it occurs?
- Is there any risk to the investigators? What has been done to mitigate this?
- Might results be skewed by inappropriate inducements?
- Will participants be aware of the experiment? Before, during, after?
- Is the experiment collecting sufficient data to give good results but not more than is needed?
- Will data about people be treated in a legal, secure and ethical manner? When will it be deleted?
- Will data about participants identify them? If so, can they request its removal?
- Will any publications using the data collected, especially pictures or internet data, allow association of individuals with the study by the reader?

It is not possible to prevent the unexpected (and if the outcome is guaranteed then what kind of experiment is it?), but it is possible to show that you have properly considered any risks and taken care of those that you identify.

2.6 Summary

In this chapter we have not presented any technique in detail, but have given reminders and pointers for a range of tools that will be useful for the lab work in the rest of the book. As a researcher or as an engineer, there is no single "correct" approach to extending the subject or better understanding our products. However, as a professional in these fields one should be aware of what approach we are taking, why we have chosen it and what the alternatives are. This applies to the choice between hypothesis, question and ethnography; to the measures we make and analysis we apply to answer our questions. These choices will inform our methods, the controls and conditions we apply, the data we collect. There are many possible solutions, and to spark ideas and then test them requires the right sort of enquiry to make progress. I wish you many revealing, exciting and enjoyable hours of research—I hope the ideas in this book will inform some of them. Having set the scene, we now delve into the issues in pervasive computing.

References

1. Clarke, G.M., Kempson, R.E.: Introduction to the Design and Analysis of Experiments. Arnold, Sevenoaks (1997)
2. Crabtree, A., Benford, S., Greenhalgh, C., Tennent, P., Chalmers, M., Brown, B.: Supporting ethnographic studies of ubiquitous computing in the wild. In: Carroll, J.M., Bødker, S., Coughlin, J. (eds.) Conference on Designing Interactive Systems, pp. 60–69. ACM, New York (2006)
3. Tufte, E.R.: The Visual Display of Quantitative Information, 2nd edn. Graphics Press, Cheshire (2001)
4. Tulloch, S. (ed.): The Oxford English Dictionary. Oxford University Press, Oxford (1995)

Part II
Systems

Chapter 3
Hardware for Pervasive Computing

There are many hardware platforms which form a part of pervasive computing: from sensors which may one day be invisible, through mobile phones to large (wall, room) interactive public systems. Along the way pervasive computing is also enabled by traditional PCs, mobile phone networks, GPS satellites and connections into existing embedded systems. To attempt an exhaustive survey here would be dull, impractical and liable to be out of date before you read the book. In this chapter we shall ignore specific details, except as an illustration of principles. Instead we shall concentrate on the issues which to a large extent define "computing" research in pervasive computing. These issues are power (Sect. 3.1), processing systems (Sect. 3.2) and networks (Sect. 3.3). However, as we shall see the underlying issues in each case are limitations in capacity, the need to scale and the variation that exists between the wide range of solutions.

The reader seeking an introduction to technical details of various hardware, systems software and programming technologies will find a book such as [2] is useful.

3.1 Power

Moore's law, where computing power (and associated with this memory capacity) increases steadily over time is be a familiar idea. However, power technology has not had the same fortune. Here we outline four of the most obvious power sources for pervasive computing: batteries, solar cells, motion generation and mains power. Each case has particular advantages and disadvantages. Other power sources exist, which you may need to consider if you engage in *systems* design, and occupy places in a similar trade-off space.

3.1.1 Batteries

Batteries are commonplace—available at the corner shop, and built into many devices which are not apparently battery powered, e.g. cars to start the engine, PC

D. Chalmers, *Sensing and Systems in Pervasive Computing*,
Undergraduate Topics in Computer Science,
DOI 10.1007/978-0-85729-841-6_3, © Springer-Verlag London Limited 2011

motherboards to keep clock time when switched off. Battery technology, compared to computing, is well established: the first made from a stack of zinc plates, paper soaked in salt water and copper and later silver plates in 1800. Modern batteries use different materials and are tidily packaged, but still rely on the principle of a chemical reaction which generates electricity and a modified chemical composition.

There is a wide range of battery technologies, each with different properties making it more or less suitable to a given situation. Key properties include:

- Nominal voltage. Most people are familiar with 1.5 volt batteries, but the actual potential depends on the cell chemistry. Voltage regulation and/or conversion can be used to match the supplied voltage to that required, but the simplest (smallest, cheapest and often most efficient and reliable) circuits are achieved where some variation can be accommodated and no voltage conversion is required. For higher voltage, cells may be combined to give multiples of the nominal voltage or charge pump circuits can be used. The latter is quite common in portable devices where the circuit is smaller and lighter than multiple cells.
- Charge capacity, typically measured in amp-hours. This is the standard rating of energy that can be supplied, but may need to be considered in light of other factors below.
- Ideal discharge patterns. Some designs are better suited to bursts of high current discharge while others are better suited to steady discharge.
- Whether or not it is rechargeable or disposable; if rechargeable what energy is required to recharge and whether it is best to recharge from fully discharged or possible to "top-up" the charge when conditions allow.
- Apparent internal resistance, and hence change in voltage under current drain. Batteries with a higher internal resistance show a reduced voltage under load. Internal resistance increases as a battery discharges, usually in a non-linear way. As a result, when tested with a high-resistance volt-meter a battery may show a higher voltage then when placed under its intended load.
- Response to temperature, most commonly a drop in voltage in the cold.
- Ability to maintain charge over time, both in terms of "shelf life" and also the behaviour under discharge-charge cycles for rechargeables.
- Physical size, which affects packaging of the device. For some applications capacity in watts per kilogram or watts per litre may be a useful measure.
- Most of these properties arise from chemical composition, which also affects its environmental impact on disposal.

So, while *Alkaline*, *Lithium Ion* and *NiMH* may be common choices and easily available it may be that a different choice is suggested for some applications. We show typical values for some of these properties in Table 3.1, although advances are still being made and specific part design and in-use loads and charging cause variation.

As battery powered hardware is often designed with a power source (or its size and price) in mind the variation in technology is experienced in the use of that power. Selection of components or power regulators may be made which reflects the drop in voltage as a battery discharges, or the range of voltages which may arise by varying the battery type.

Table 3.1 A comparison of common battery technologies' typical performance from [3, 7, 10] and various data sheets

Type	Cell voltage (V)	Energy density (Wh/l)	Specific power (Wh/kg)	Self discharge (%/month)	Charge Cycles (number)	Other features
Lead Acid	2.1	60–75	20–40	3	500	high peak current, good low temperature performance, faster self-discharge at high temperature
Li Ion	3.6	250–360	100–250	5	1200	
Li Pol	3.7	300	130–200	5	1000	
NiCd	1.2	50–150	40–60	30	900	memory effect if not fully discharged
NiMH	1.2	140–300	30–90	60	400	
Alkaline	1.5	300	110	<1	non-rechargeable	
Zinc-air	1.65	900	300–400	<1	non-rechargeable, usually button cells	

Software designed to be portable across devices might have to understand its expected time to next charge, its current power capacity and budget accordingly. Laptop PC operating systems are becoming power aware as a first step in achieving this, but generally this is limited to reducing power consumption when idle and making the user aware of the power level; actively managing energy use is still at quite a basic level. Sensor network routing algorithms sometimes consider power availability, typically by moving communal burdens onto those nodes most able to cope and so extending the lifetime of the complete network.

Despite their widespread use batteries have some significant limitations: They contain a limited charge and either need recharging or replacing when this is gone. In order to extend this lifetime larger, higher powered, and to a limited extent alternative chemistry, more expensive, batteries may be used. However, bulky batteries do not make for devices which physically "disappear". More importantly, batteries which are actively used without a disappearing recharging process (i.e. through their natural use like a car battery), do not allow their use to scale to large numbers of devices as the burden of manual battery maintenance would be prohibitive. Even today this is an issue: you do not have to travel far by public transport to hear someone explaining that they need to be quick because their mobile phone battery is almost flat; in the UK government statistics for 2007 [1] show that over 2000 battery operated smoke alarms failed to raise the alarm in a fire due to missing or flat batteries; [5] reports that in cases of accidental deaths due to fire in the home in London between 1996–2000 one third of smoke alarms fitted were not operating due to missing or flat batteries. If a single device in daily use (and conforming to the subconscious / tool-like use of pervasive computing) cannot be maintained, creating many additional devices seems ill-fated.

We shall now outline three other power sources. However, in each case we shall see batteries proposed as part of those solutions.

3.1.2 Solar Cells

Solar cells have been available for some time, and have experienced significant development driven by the needs of satellites and more recently as alternative power sources become a more mainstream idea. At a basic level solar powered calculators have been available since the late 1970s. As for batteries there is a size vs. power capacity trade-off to consider. As a sole power source there is an obvious power limitation, of requiring significant light levels to function. The light level also causes a significant variation in power produced. As a result of these two factors solar cells are often used to charge batteries, which smooths the consumption and generation mis-match. Another application is as a dedicated battery charger, for situations where mains power is not available for this duty. Of course some devices cannot have guaranteed regular exposure to light, but in reality many lower-power consumption devices could use solar cells with only slight enlargement to accommodate the solar cells. In order to scale to more widespread use continued improvements in power generation for low light levels and small sizes at reasonable costs are required to make solar cells more widely applicable.

3.1.3 Motion Generators

Motion generators are rather less widely used for computing than solar power, but are seen as having significant potential for devices which are mobile—and therefore presumably being moved on a regular basis. Motion generators as a term encompasses a wide range of technology, typically by the motion of magnets around coils e.g. a bicycle dynamo, or wind-up radio; or piezo-electric generation, for instance built into the heel of shoes. In both cases there are some practical limits to consider in terms of the level of power that can be generated without turning the device into an exercise machine. As for solar cells there is a size vs. power capacity trade-off; and issues with the variation in available power between different users and at different times. Again, some power storage may be necessary, to allow function when not generating—particularly when walking or turning a handle would impede the use of the device. For some devices the requirement that someone engage in physical activity to generate power is a significant limitation, but these technologies may well form part of the spectrum of power sources—particularly for wearable computing.

3.1.4 Mains Power

Mains (grid) power is often ruled out early in pervasive computing design, and with good reason: it requires wires and mobility is often part of the system deign assumptions. However, there is the assumption that rechargeable batteries can be recharged, for which mains power is a common source of energy. There are some developments in providing energy wirelessly, by induction in the short range or microwave and laser over longer (but line of sight) range. The most familiar of these is probably the inductive charging of electric toothbrushes, where avoiding exposed electrical contacts in a wet environment, rather than making the device distant from cables, is the main advantage. The range and efficiency of these approaches mean that they are not in widespread use as a means of avoiding cables at present, but are an active area of research and consumer products may well adopt these technologies in the near future. For consumer devices this technology also offers a means to reduce the number of different mains chargers, each with a different connector and a fragile cable, that one needs to maintain phones, PDAs, cameras, MP3 players, e-books etc.

Despite assumptions of mobility much of the infrastructure of pervasive computing does or could make use of mains wired devices: wireless network base stations, servers, sensors built into the fabric of a building etc. Mains electricity has already disappeared into the background to user consciousness. Mains power has an advantage over local sources in scalability, but places burdens on flexibility (constant or regular need for static power sources) and design constraints on devices, which must be sited near a power source or incorporate transformers and regulators to turn the high voltage AC into the more usable (for computing electronics) low voltage DC. In some cases mains power becomes a reasonable assumption, although greater problems are experienced when siting large amounts of new equipment in older buildings; if unlimited energy is assumed then we must also consider the heat generated, the noise from fans, the environmental cost of generation; and finally—what happens when the power fails?

3.1.5 Power: Summary

There is not one ideal energy source. As we have seen, storing energy is an important principle in order to cover periods when energy generation is not possible. Battery technology will develop, but historically it has lagged behind increases in computing's ability to drain power. It is only through careful management of resources and adaptation to variation in the availability of power that pervasive computing can scale. The adaptation may involve delaying work until spare resource is available or modifying expectations, producing lower quality solutions when necessary (building on the idea of compression to reduce storage space for images). The scale is both in terms of device numbers, but more importantly the ability to keep them running for a long time without change or manual charging of batteries, to make the effort and environmental costs of a solution acceptable.

3.2 Processing

We mentioned Moore's law above and a commonplace assumption in computing research is that you can imagine rather more CPU power being available by the time you have finished a project than when you start. This increase in computing power comes through a combination of effects: more complex CPUs (specialised instructions, deeper pipelines, speculative execution), faster clock speeds, greater parallelism (deeper pipelines, multiple cores), more memory (caches, main memory and special purpose memory for graphics etc.), and faster peripherals to match. However, to a greater or lesser extent, each of these advantages requires more energy—which as we saw above makes blanket assumptions that more computing power will be available a deeply flawed assumption for pervasive computing (and, in environmental terms, all computing). Of course, we also do not wish to define pervasive computing as simply turning back time on computing. To find a solution we will look at some of the components in more depth to see what can be done across a complete system design.

3.2.1 CPUs

There are a few typical choices in CPUs made in pervasive computing: to use a variant on general purpose computer technology, as for laptops; to use a somewhat specialised CPU with sufficient power, as in mobile phones; or to treat the design as a low-power embedded computing project, as for sensor network nodes. In the case of mobile phones one must consider that there are multiple processing units, including digital signal processor (DSP) architectures for radio and audio processing and more traditional processors for the user interface (now moving from simple embedded architectures to more powerful processors to handle more visual interfaces and complex applications). Below, we briefly examine some key architectural considerations. A sample of processor types and currently available specifications is shown in Table 3.2.

The need for *support components* might not be the most obvious first parameter, but it has a significant impact on system design. If a chosen CPU comes with program and data memory, analogue to digital converters, serial ports etc built into a single package then the size and manufacturing complexity of the final design will be much lower than the general purpose CPU for which supporting components must be chosen from many options and configured as needed. These classifications are essentially that of "micro-controller" and "micro-processor" respectively, although the boundary can be blurred. The trade-off here is whether the simplicity proves limiting and requires greater device specific code compilation than a more general purpose approach.

Clock speed is, as any good computer architecture course will tell you, little more than a marketing tool. It tells you how often a unit of work is done, but to compare CPUs you must also understand what work is done in that unit. However, for a given architecture it is generally the case that work done and power consumed per unit time are both functions of clock speed. For many CPUs, particularly micro-controllers, clock speed may be varied down to DC which allows power consumption to be controlled where use of CPU "sleep" states would be problematic.

The number of *bits* in the main data bus in a CPU is an important consideration: it limits the default size of numbers; it is usually reflected in (but not always equal to-) the width of the memory bus; the memory address bus is usually a low multiple (e.g. 2) of this size and so limits the practical memory size. Much of embedded computing works with 8 bit memory and main ALU sizes, some limited support for 16 bit arithmetic, and 16 bit memory addresses. 8 bits is sufficient to represent many physical phenomena with human range and precision; it is sufficient to encode ASCII text and 64k bytes of memory is sufficient to hold a reasonably complex control system. Indeed, for a micro-controller this value is not shown as a choice parameter on some popular component suppliers—which "family" of devices they are part of (which implies a bus width, often 8 bit), I/O support (including ADC, DAC, PWM, and particular serial busses), internal program and data memory sizes and types, and supply voltage ranges are more normal choice parameters—hence the much larger number of options seen in Table 3.2. Of course, in general purpose computing 8 bits ceased to be sufficient a long time ago, and for user interfaces which process complex graphics a larger memory and straightforward floating-point arithmetic support (which both imply more bits) are needed; for processing large bodies of text or long data histories greater data memory is needed; for more complex programs (with greater structure and general purpose functionality) more program memory is needed. The "correct" size therefore depends on the application, although the choice may be limited as shown in Table 3.2.

In "traditional" computing CISC and RISC *CPU architectures* used to be significant issue. For current general purpose computing *x86* compatibility is currently the norm, which implies a CISC (with some RISC influence) von-Neumann architecture. For specialised processors for audio, video and radio a DSP architecture is most appropriate. For embedded processors both von-Neumann and Harvard architectures are commonplace, although because they infrequently change their programs and even more rarely compile code for themselves the separation of program and data store of a Harvard architecture is quite practical. For more complex embedded systems and general purpose designs the system architecture will generally include memory management systems, providing for virtual address spaces and special privileges for operating system code.

CPU architecture limits, in particular Arithmetic and Logic Unit (ALU) limits, have an increasing impact on programming style the closer design gets to simple embedded CPUs. A typical PC programmer spends very little time considering how high level language code maps to machine instructions—this is, in some respects, the point of high level languages. However, with some of the more limited architectures we are considering it makes sense for the programmer to be more aware of whether underlying support for floating point can be assumed and the speed and

Table 3.2 CPU design parameters, an example of the range as available at the time of writing from one supplier, does not include PC parts

Class	Bits	Max. Freq. (MHz)	No. diff. parts
Microprocessor	8	4–55	1
	10	48	1
	16	10–25	2
	32	–	201
	of which	8–100	62
		100–1000	136
		1–1.3 GHz	3
Micro-controller	–	–	3023
	of which	32 kHz–10 MHz	663
		10–100	2327
		100–400	33
DSP	–	–	137
	16	10–100	27
	16	100–500	13
	24	180–275	5
	32	60–600	12
	not given	10–100	9
		100–600	71

energy impacts of using more complex operators accommodated. This awareness can be as simple as whether there are better choices of data type for some variables than int or float; better choices of instruction than *2 (i.e. shift); or choosing algorithms which use fewer operations, fewer branches, fewer intermediate variables etc.

CPU choice interacts with programs to produce outputs and also heat. Switching transistors and driving outputs causes a CPU to *consume power*, switching more transistors faster consumes more power, changes in transistor deign (in particular gate threshold voltage) changes power consumption. Some architectures may have a larger power drain just by being on or for a given code sequence than others. Some architectures may have ways of reducing their power consumption: by slowing the clock, or introducing sleep states (to be woken after a time or on some other interrupt), or switching off parts of their circuits. The ideal processor for a given program must obviously be powerful enough to execute the program within the available time, and as a rule of thumb the lowest power consumption will be from a simple slow architecture. Within the CPUs satisfying these conditions, depending on the nature of the program the right choice might depend on what happens in the "slack" time and how much of this time there is—rather than a headline current drain.

Table 3.3 Memory type parameters, an example of the range as available at the time of writing, does not include PC parts

Class	Max size (Mb)	Typ. current standby, active (mA)	Access time (ns)	Notes
DRAM	256	30, 180	5–17	volatile
SRAM	18	20, 90	8–150	volatile
EEPROM	1024	0.1, 40	50–250 (for read)	non-volatile most 5 V not 3 V
Flash	4096	0.025, 10–19 (read), 18 (write)	45–250	non-volatile
FRAM	2048	0.01, 15	100	non-volatile

3.2.2 Memory

Finally, we should consider memory—sometimes integral to the CPU chip, but not always—which affects how we handle power and how we handle data. Here again we find ourselves considering speed and power consumption, but also size and volatility. We mentioned von Neumann and Harvard architectures before, but the distinction between program and data memory handling is worth considering, even in traditional computing where disk partitions, network storage, and disk / memory / cache residency affect performance. In the more embedded side of pervasive computing program changes are infrequent enough that speed and power consumption to make these changes can be secondary to stability and low running power consumption, hence the frequent choice of EEPROM and Flash for these purposes. In a battery powered device recovering from a power loss must be assumed. Some working data can be lost without harm, other configuration and long-term record data must be handled in other ways. Where read frequently SRAM or a copy from EEPROM to volatile memory is a practical choice to balance speed and reliability. Where data is being recorded and must survive power interruptions, other stores such as Flash, ferro-electric RAM (FRAM), and off-device store (disk, network) are also possibilities depending on cost, hardware complexity read / write patterns and data volume restrictions. That data can be stored off-device, especially over the network, is important to remember. A summary of memory types and their key properties is shown in Table 3.3. Indeed, in sensor networks very little data need be stored on any node as their primary purpose is to move data out to consumers. Where very "thin" clients are considered then moving processing to proxies and data store to servers is similarly natural.

3.2.3 Processing: Summary

Pervasive computing does not require that we attach a battery to computers from the 1980s. Modern ideas are integral to success here and current trends in mobile phones, netbooks and wireless networks are finding success. But, it does require several things from us in system design:

- To take care with resources used in programming, by applying suitable compiler optimisations but also through resource awareness in software engineering.
- To consider the distribution of code as using more than homogeneous black boxes. Some nodes will be limited, some nodes will fail, communication costs are significant.
- Hardware design may need to avoid the latest components in some places and to negotiate software requirements down in order to gain efficiency.
- Packaging design must consider cooling without fans and accommodating batteries and charging solutions.

As before: there is no one "best" type of CPU architecture, memory etc. Different devices will have different limitations, designing with awareness of these limitations and accommodating the variation are important principles.

3.3 Conclusions

Many researchers have developed solutions to hardware choice in pervasive computing, e.g. [6]. New approaches to design, new applications and new components will undoubtedly give rise to further alternatives. None of these is "correct"—each makes a choice in the available design space, with different trade-offs. Each rightly accepts certain limitations in order to fit their requirements, a one architecture fits all approach (as adopted in the desktop PC arena) is not appropriate here. The limitations are important. The limitations may become less severe over time, as technology advances. However. the power and size requirements of pervasive computing will mean that it remains limited compared to desktop computing. Probably more important that the limitations however are the variations—in each place in the architecture. How software handles these variations to enable re-usability, how architectures and protocols handle these variations, and whether programmers are aware of the scope of variation will be key to success in tackling effective engineering for such devices.

You may have noticed a chapter on networks follows (Chap. 4). This has been given a separate chapter as communication is so central to pervasive computing and networking more commonly a "software" subject than hardware choice is. In this you will find a rather more detailed review of the issues which make networks in pervasive computing interesting to the computer scientist. It will quickly become apparent that the themes of this chapter: working with limitations, making appropriate choices for particular systems and expecting and accommodating variation can be applied to networks as well.

3.4 Suggested Readings

- Students studying computing might like to review their own introductory notes on computer architecture and system design.
- Weiser's initial review of issues, including hardware, which are significant in pervasive computing Mark Weiser. Some computer science issues in ubiquitous computing. *Communications of the ACM*, 36(7):75–84, 1993
- A discussion of sensor network platforms Jason Hill, Mike Horton, Ralph Kling, and Lakshman Krishnamurthy. The platforms enabling wireless sensor networks. *Commun. ACM*, 47:41–46, June 2004
- This paper is not a discussion of hardware, but addresses similar themes to this chapter in addressing variation in software and managing energy use Mahadev Satyanarayanan. Pervasive computing: Vision and challenges. *IEEE Personal Communications*, 8(4):10–17, 2001.

3.5 Laboratory Exercises: Algorithm Profiling

In learning to program on a modern PC memory use is often neglected as a consideration and speed is only considered if the user interface is slow. Start to consider CPU cycles and memory as a finite resource.

1. Take some familiar algorithms, e.g. different sorting techniques, and use profiling tools to compare them:
   (a) Which uses the most memory?
   (b) Review each algorithm to see whether memory use can be reduced by more efficient data structures.
   (c) How can run-time be reduced for the sorting algorithm?
   (d) Identify any network or disk accesses taking place during execution, how can these be avoided?
2. Generate a set of inputs from a sensor, possibly recorded from the Phidgets lab in Chap. 1. Process these to generate an exponentially weighted moving average: $avg_n = 0.125 * reading + 0.875 * avg_{n-1}$. See how hand-optimisations change the results in terms of memory or CPU time (you may need quite a large set of values or to repeat several times). Consider what state you maintain between inputs, whether alternative ALU operations might be more efficient, what the implication of changing data types is. This may be easier with C or assembler but you should be able to arrange some variations in performance with Java. If you cannot find improvements, can you find ways in which a less skilled programmer might have made a slower / more memory hungry program; or consider a more complex algorithm?

References

1. Fire statistics, United Kingdom, 2007. Technical report, Department for Communities and Local Government (2007)

2. Hansmann, U., Merk, L., Nicklous, M.S., Stober, T.: Pervasive Computing Handbook. Springer, Berlin (2001)
3. Higgins, K.: New technology batteries guide. Technical Report NIJ Guide 200-98, National Institute of Justice, National Law Enforcement and Corrections Technology Center (1998)
4. Hill, J., Horton, M., Kling, R., Krishnamurthy, L.: The platforms enabling wireless sensor networks. Commun. ACM 47, 41–46 (2004)
5. Holborn, P.G.: Fire deaths in London 1996–2000. Technical report, South Bank University for London Fire and Emergency Planning Authority (2001)
6. Holmquist, L.E., Gellersen, H.-W., Kortuem, G., Schmidt, A., Strohbach, M., Antifakos, S., Michahelles, F., Schiele, B., Beigl, M., Mazé, R.: Building intelligent environments with smart-its. IEEE Comput. Graph. Appl. 24(1), 56–64 (2004)
7. Horowitz, P., Hill, W.: The Art of Electronics. Cambridge University Press, New York (1989)
8. Satyanarayanan, M.: Pervasive computing: vision and challenges. IEEE Pers. Commun. 8(4), 10–17 (2001)
9. Weiser, M.: Some computer science issues in ubiquitous computing. Commun. ACM 36(7), 75–84 (1993)
10. Wikipedia: Batteries. http://en.wikipedia.org/wiki/Category:Battery_(electricity). Accessed September 2010

Chapter 4
Networks

In this chapter we shall examine some key issues and principles that arise in networking for pervasive computing. As for hardware we shall not attempt to be complete or current in our coverage here, but to extract a basis for understanding and a starting point for further learning. There is a wide range of textbooks, standards and research papers on networking which the interested reader can move on to. It is easy to imagine that all the networks in pervasive computing are wireless, and that is certainly a common assumption, but wired infrastructure still plays a part. The range of possibilities and issues is great, so before we examine detail we shall touch on some basic categorisation. The range of choices available in each category gives rise to an interesting engineering challenge and the need to cater for variation in systems design [3].

4.1 Patterns of Movement and Connectivity

Mobile systems can be categorised by patterns of movement and connectivity.

- *Fixed* devices are those which are generally stationary in the network topology, connecting to particular ports in a wired network infrastructure, e.g. desktop PCs and mains control devices embedded in buildings.
- *Nomadic devices* move from place to place, being used in those places but not in a seamless fashion. Network connections are explicitly formed in new locations, typically connecting through local area networks or dial-up services.
- *Nomadic users* move from place to place, using different (probably fixed) devices in those places. Their data may follow them from place to place, or they may hand-replicate configurations in each place. Again, the experience is not seamless.
- *Mobile* connection requires devices that move freely (along with users) with largely automatic negotiation of connection during movement and rare changes in network performance, e.g. mobile phones.

Patterns of movement give rise to relationships between devices and data, and affect the range of contexts the user will have to work in. Patterns of connectivity

D. Chalmers, *Sensing and Systems in Pervasive Computing*,
Undergraduate Topics in Computer Science,
DOI 10.1007/978-0-85729-841-6_4, © Springer-Verlag London Limited 2011

establish different approaches to managing networks and choosing the most appropriate media. Approaching seamless experience requires not only automated access, but also any payment for that access, a widespread deployment of devices to afford connectivity, and management of the quality of service (QoS) of the network.

As well as patterns of movement it is also useful to consider the physical scope of a network: how far apart are terminals and hence how far can mobile and nomadic devices move while still being able to connect to the network. The coverage of networks is commonly characterised as:

- *Wide Area Network* (WAN)—covering a wide area, characterised by long distance connections often run over telecommunications provider or internet service provider infrastructure, although larger organisations may have dedicated facilities. Technologies include leased lines, frame relay and SONET/SDH. On a *metropolitan* scale (MAN) a slightly different trade off between speed and distance can be made. IEEE 802.16, also known as "WiMAX" is an emerging standard for wireless broadband on this scale. Cellular telephone networks can be used to carry data. They are quite local in the connection to the base station but are generally used as part of a wide area network. The connection from the base station is typically wired, although point-to-point microwave links may be used too.
- *Local Area Network* (LAN)—local being relative to a wide area network, typically contained within a building or collection of buildings and also typically dedicated to a single organisation. The various classes of Ethernet (IEEE 802.3) and wireless LAN (IEEE 802.11, also known as "WiFi") are the most common technologies today.
- A *Vehicle Area Network* (VAN) describes a network contained within a vehicle. They are typically wired and characterised by a need for very reliable communications for real-time safety critical functions and stable, well tested configurations.
- A *Personal Area Network* (PAN) describes a network formed from devices on and about a person. This may include PDAs, mobile phones, wireless headsets, smart clothes and devices nearby but not owned by the person in question that the network includes to achieve certain functions, such as PCs and printers. IEEE 802.15 family standards are typical, with Bluetooth and ZigBee (802.15.4) being the most widely used.
- A *Body Area Network* (BAN) is characterised by devices worn on or embedded within the body. Typical uses are for medical applications, although it may also provide for secure identity data. Signals may be conducted by the body, or use very low power wireless for health reasons. Connection outside the body may be intermittent, for instance to download diagnostic data during medical intervention.

In this chapter we will focus on LAN and PAN technologies and issues, but the principles discussed are often applicable to other classes of networks and some situations will require considering wider range or specialised considerations of other cases.

4.2 Radio Networks Overview

Networks vary in the media they use to connect devices: guided ("wired") electrical and electromagnetic, e.g. optical, signals and unguided ("wireless") electromagnetic and audio signals. Wired media include mains electrical cables, twisted pair, coaxial cable and fibre optics; these either carry electrical signals or guide electromagnetic waves. Wireless media includes: radio; targeted lasers, e.g. between rooftops; and infra-red. Radio includes directional micro-wave; licensed bands of omnidirectional radio (as for audio programmes); and low power industrial, scientific and medical (ISM) bands. Audio for communications is generally ultrasonic. Each approach has its own properties: distance between repeaters, ease of set-up, ease of eavesdropping, energy required, achievable bandwidth, susceptibility to environmental effects etc.

4.2.1 Bands and Bandwidth

To transmit data a radio signal is modified: in frequency, amplitude or phase. The duration for which that signal state is maintained is the symbol rate. If there are two signal states, e.g. high–low, then one data bit can be sent per symbol state. In modern schemes a greater number of signal states are often possible, allowing a data rate which is greater than the symbol rate: $data\_rate = symbol\_states/symbol\_duration$ Faster signal rates take a wider band as the band taken is determined by the fastest signal change when combined with the carrier wave. Most radio protocols use frequency or phase modulation rather than varying duration signals, which helps to keep a constant clock simple. Additionally on-off keying is quite inefficient and complex to detect as signal strength drops, so frequency or phase modulation are often used rather than amplitude.

Different radio frequencies have different properties. We describe the broadest scale bands in Table 4.1. The properties include:

• Whether the signal propagates over the horizon
• The size of antenna required for efficient communications
• The complexity of the electronics and shielding required
• Susceptibility to reflection, and therefore multi-path reflection (which can affect achievable data rate)

Within each section of the spectrum there are locally licensed allocations, including in some cases unlicensed ISM bands and amateur radio bands, which have publicly available licences for shared use. The ISM bands are commonly used for computer communications and further require that protocols tolerate interference and that devices conform to requirements for limited radiated radio energy. The allocated bands vary in width, determined by demand and the complexity of producing radios which take advantage of the full band without going outside the allocated range. Within these bands it is also possible to have channels, which sub-divide the allocation into

Table 4.1 Radio frequency bands and use

Band	Frequency	Uses
VLF, LF	3–300 kHz	Maritime, time signals, simple beacons, RFID
MF	300 kHz–3 MHz	AM, coax, twisted pair
HF	3–30 MHz	Lowest over horizon radio, short-wave radio, over-horizon radar, RFID, radio-telephones
VHF	30–300 MHz	FM radio, twisted pair wired use ends
UHF	300 MHz–3 GHz	TV, wired coax use ends, ZigBee, GPS, Bluetooth, microwave ovens
	865 MHz, 915 MHz, 2.450 GHz	ISM bands used in various wireless networks
	880–915 MHz, 935–960 MHz	GSM-900 telephony
	1.71–1.785 GHz, 1.805–1.88 GHz	GSM-1800 telephony
	1.92–1.98 GHz, 2.11–2.17 GHz	UMTS-2100 3G telephony
SHF	3–30 GHz	Satellite, radar, wireless LAN
	5.80 GHz	ISM band used in some IEEE 802.11 wireless LANs
EHF	30–300 GHz	Microwave links

practical units of use. These channels may not be legislated, but adopted by one of the various standards using the band. Channels might allow different frequencies for up and down links in a scheme with a base station, or for overlapping cells of communication.

While efficient use of a band is desirable many modern communications systems, including IEEE 802.11, use *spread spectrum* techniques such as Direct Sequence Spread Spectrum (DSSS) and Frequency Hopping. Here the data signal is spread across the full width of the allocated channel. This provides additional resilience against jamming, interference and environmental effects, e.g. multi-path fading. In many cases these techniques require accurate synchronisation of sender and receiver, to ensure that changes in frequency (frequency hopping) or selection of chipping sequence (DSSS) do not result in loss of data.

The environment, transmitted power, antenna design and properties of radio for a given band determine the propagation of the signal. In general, over-powered radios use batteries faster, prevent others communicating but don't send their own data any faster. Of course under-powered radios suffer from interference and will typically have to repeat messages lost due to interference. Most standards (and often legal restrictions too) determine limits on transmitted power, which balance efficiency and coverage *for the intended application*. Above we considered the spectral capacity of radios, where choice of modulation affects use of the frequency spectrum. For the dense networking envisaged for pervasive computing we should also consider the *spatial capacity* of our networks, although a single figure can obscure more complex issues. For instance IEEE 802.11 g has a capacity of up to 400 kb/s/m^2 at a 54 Mb/s data rate while Bluetooth has 25 kb/s/m^2 at a 1 Mb/s data rate [7]. The wireless LAN standard is designed for communications on a home / office scale and has a data rate and channel sharing systems to suit. The PAN standard has a shorter range and background lower power demands and the capacity of the LAN standard falls as the data rate falls. The overheads of organising independent communications and constraints on the number of overlapping cells would prevent effective use of 802.11 in a PAN application—only four independent networks each with a 100 m can be supported in IEEE 802.11, while Bluetooth allows twenty networks with a 10 m range. To achieve longer range communications use of shared infrastructure and gateways between network types will be needed [20]. We return to these issues in Sect. 4.5.

4.2.2 Access

There are various challenges to communications created by wireless networks, that are generally avoided in wired networks with well defined transmission power. Having outlined the idea of choice around propagation and speed in wireless networks, which gives rise to a range of radio technology choices. We shall now consider the challenges raised in relation to establishing communications using wireless networks. These still refer to radio propagation, but we start to move up the protocol stack and consider the link layer in finding solutions.

When we discussed spatial capacity above we glossed over the details of radio interfaces—this is a subject in its own right and better tackled in its own setting with the appropriate physics and electronics to back it up. However, even in our limited setting the idea of range can usefully be expanded into three categories:

- Reception range
- Detection range
- Interference range

Up until now we have focused on *reception range*—where useful communications takes place. However it is useful to consider when a signal can be detected and when a signal may interfere with another signal, even if it is not directly detected. When considering spatial capacity the interference range determines the density of transmitters.

Non-symmetric paths are illustrated in Fig. 4.1. In a well functioning network (at top of figure) the sender and receiver are within each others' reception zone. (This zone is a function of sender power and receiver sensitivity, but we have drawn as a zone around a node in which that node can be received from for simplicity.) Where the two have the same power output, no restrictions in direction due to antenna design, and the same receiver sensitivity this is easy to arrange. Where one node is less capable, e.g. has a weaker battery or less sophisticated antenna, the reception zones are not equally sized. In this case it becomes easier for one node to be able to send but not to receive (directly) from the other.

We are particularly interested in interference in the use of radio as, typically, only one of reception and transmission occur at a time, as the transmitted signal would overwhelm any other signals. For this reason we also assume that communications are half-duplex, even if they are bi-directional. In a wired network, such as Ethernet, a transmitter can reasonably "listen" while transmitting and detect any other transmissions occurring at the same time. So, in a wired network where the medium is shared a Carrier Sense Multiple Access with Collision Detection (CSMA/CD) protocol can be used—where a node wishing to transmit tests for other transmissions, if none are found starts to transmit. Because propagation delay is finite a collision may still occur, but can be detected by the transmitter by comparing transmitted and received signals. This approach cannot be used in a wireless network, so different approaches must be taken: Firstly in planned deployments spatially overlapping use of channels is avoided. If central control is possible multiple stations can exist in the same region by dividing channels further, e.g. with frequency, time or code division multiplex schemes. This approach is common in telephony, but less so in computer networking where less control is assumed. The alternative approach is Carrier Sense Multiple Access with Collision Avoidance (CSMA/CA). Here the protocol is designed to avoid collisions occurring, as the overhead of discovering collisions and re-transmissions is high and so a small loss of efficiency to avoid this work can be tolerated. Of course collisions are only avoided, and such protocols typically include acknowledgement (ACK) signals into their protocols to confirm the correct reception of data. This approach also allows for the inherent variation in quality that occurs in wireless networks. Before presenting the detail of such a scheme we shall illustrate how easily the situation arises.

Referring to Fig. 4.1, in the *hidden terminal problem* nodes S1 and S2 can both see R, but not each other. Therefore S1 cannot tell when S2 is transmitting, and vice-versa. However if they transmit at the same time, on the same channel the signals will interfere with each other at R and neither set of data will be received correctly—indeed, the identity of the transmitters cannot in general be known. Possible fixes include: increase power or improve receivers at S1, S2; move S1 and/or S2 relative to each other or any obstructions or improve radio so that they can *detect* each other; and have a scheme where S1 and S2 avoid collisions, typically by engaging R in a negotiation for rights to transmit. If S1 requests to send (RTS) and R clears to send (CTS), S2 should hear the CTS directed at S1 and wait. RTS signals may still collide, but a lack of CTS can prompt a further RTS—with an appropriate random delay to avoid repeating the collision. If

$$detectionrange > 2 * receptionrange \qquad (4.1)$$

then it becomes hard to arrange hidden terminals without physical obstructions to signal propagation.

In the *exposed terminal problem* we have four nodes, and this time the senders can detect each other. S2 believes it will interfere if it sends at the same time as S1 although the two receivers will not get an interfered with signal as R1 is out of interference range of S2 and similarly for R2 and S1. Possible solutions include: reduce power at S1 and S2 to move out of each others detection range (while still being in reception range for the corresponding R); more directional antennae; erect a barrier between S1 and S2; or make use of a protocol where S1 and S2 engage

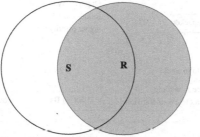

Two nodes, in range of each other: successful communication

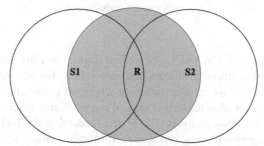

S1 and S2 both in range of R: hidden terminal problem

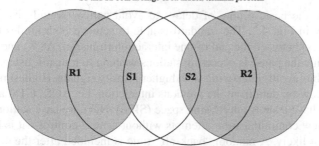

S1can send to R1, S2 can send to R2, but S1 and S2 detect each other: exposed terminal problem

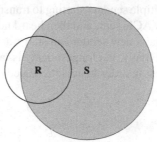

S sends to R, but R cannot send to S: asymmetric path problem

Fig. 4.1 Paths in wireless networks

R1 and R2 in understanding propagation. If S1 and S2 listen for each-others control signals then S1 will hear S2's RTS, but not corresponding CTS from R2, and will know transmission is OK (assuming equal strength signals).

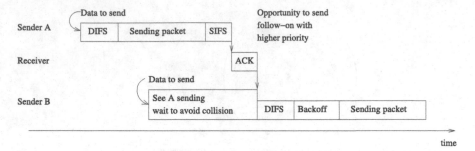

Fig. 4.2 Illustration of 802.11 DCF carrier sense multiple access / collision avoidance medium access timing

IEEE 802.11 uses a CSMA/CA scheme and thus allows for both the hidden terminal and exposed terminal problems and also allows for base-station control of who transmits when—this cellular structure where all communication takes place via a central controller also removes many of the problems discussed here. On the other hand, in a simulated analysis [22] it was found that the lack of RTS/CTS in IEEE 802.15.4 gave rise to a measurable performance penalty arising from hidden terminals.

We illustrate the basic timing of delays to avoid collisions and give different stations priority in Fig. 4.2. The standard is able to achieve both modes by using pauses (or spaces) between the end of one interaction (transmit, ACK) and the start of the next. While the pause is occurring stations wishing to transmit listen, in order to detect (and thus avoid) interfering with higher priority signals. Highest priority is control and follow-on data from the previous interaction, i.e. ACK, CTS, and next-packets, which have a short inter-frame space (SIFS). Next are base station control frames. Then new communication attempts without central control—it is here that collision is most likely. A random "back-off" time is included after the distributed Inter-frame space (DIFS) delay in this case, to ensure that follow-on frames get priority and to avoid multiple senders starting to transmit at the same time. If, having heard a packet finish, an ACK sent, and then heard no transmissions after waiting a DIFS and a back-off time a new sender can start transmitting (as is the case in our illustration in Fig. 4.2. Finally, the longest delay is taken by those recovering from error. The delay is longest in order to avoid repeated errors blocking other access to the medium.

4.2.3 Error

Detecting and correcting errors is as important for wireless network and sensor network protocols as in other applications. The usual schemes: backward error correction, e.g. through check-sums; forward error correction through greater redundancy; providing for graceful degradation; and ACK and negative acknowledgement (NACK) messages remain useful. In some sensor network applications loss can be tolerated, and we return to this later. However, in wireless networks the overhead of error detection and correction has a significant impact:

- Errors due to interference are often bursty, altering some assumptions about how useful error correction data is and making immediate re-transmission unreliable. It may be better to reduce overheads wait until successful packet reception has been reestablished before re-transmitting lost data.
- Sending acknowledgements incurs additional opportunities for collision, so where possible cumulative ACKs and combination of ACKs across protocol layers should be implemented. IEEE 802.11 gives priority to such messages to avoid collisions.
- Sending additional protocol messages and redundant data has energy and spatial capacity costs, which are often significant in pervasive computing.

Given the costs of additional data for error detection, correction, and re-transmission other approaches must be given consideration in pervasive computing. The TCP approach of desktop computing may not be the most appropriate for use in mobile, ad-hoc networks. In particular, one must consider whether some error or loss can be accommodated in streams of sensed data, and filtered in the same way as other sources of error. Also, designing applications to withstand disconnections, changes of network identity, and loss of packets is important. A connection less, stateless approach is often more desirable when considering fragile, transient communications than it might be for traditional client–server paradigm applications.

4.2.4 Energy Efficient Networks

The energy cost of networks depends a lot on the particular system in use, considering: amplification circuits, antenna design and protocol design. However, when considering the power budget for a system wireless networks are typically one of the most significant components. The figures vary from case to case, three studies are suggested in the readings: [6, 14] and [21]. However, each of the following has a power cost:

- Transmitting (usually the most significant)
- Receiving
- Listening (often not much less than actually receiving)
- Turning the radio on

In order to reduce the cost of the most significant components protocols should be designed which reduce bit count, compress large bodies of data (unless the energy cost to the CPU exceeds the saved network costs) and most significantly reducing the number of protocol messages used to achieve a task.

Although transmission takes the most energy, it is not uncommon for listening to take at least half this power, so putting radio circuits to sleep is desirable. In sensor networks protocols are often designed around *scheduled* transmission, enabling radios to be switched off for well defined periods. Care needs to be taken over the time and energy required to turn the radio on again in determining a lower bound for the off time. Scheduling periods of sleep is also complex: many pervasive computing systems react to unpredictable events, so a long sleep delays response; and in simple low-power circuits clock accuracy is sometimes not the best, so that some flexibility must be built into the wake-up timing.

For the content of this book, the most significant contribution to savings is in reducing the volume of data communicated—saving network bandwidth and energy and possibly in application protocol design—does a message really need to be sent? The impact of energy saving mechanisms must also be considered: transmission may be delayed or dropped to save energy, e.g. in passing on sensor readings, leading to a need to produce tolerant software designs. The interested reader might want to start with [11], which although 10 years old as this is written gives a good introduction to energy efficiency issues across the whole protocol stack.

4.2.5 Security

Wireless communication differs from wired in the ease of interception. Physical access controls to network ports are possible with a wired network, but very difficult for wireless networks. Detecting eavesdropping is similarly difficult. So, security requires that:

- Signal propagation is limited. For wireless infrastructure this may be by choosing location and power of access points; for mobile devices this may be by choosing appropriate locations from which to connect.
- Appropriate access controls to joining the network infrastructure should be used, such as MAC address registration and network login with passwords or physical tokens such as SIM cards.
- Data is encrypted. Although the strength of encryption in many protocols is limited it is sufficient to deter the casual observer and for establishing connections. Additional application layer encryption should also be used where appropriate.
- Patterns of communication should not be revealing where privacy is important. Patterns of movement, communication partners and correlation with other data should all be considered.

A further consideration is the idea of *identity* in pervasive computing. This is an active research area, and we only outline the issues here. People may:

- Share devices and infrastructure, e.g. computers and networks at home and work.
- Own multiple devices, e.g. laptops, phones etc.
- Move between networks frequently, e.g. home, mobile, coffee shop, work, friends homes.
- Have multiple identities, e.g. email addresses or social network IDs for work, shopping, friends, family, hobbies.

Where pervasive applications require user identity these issues must be considered. A device may store state and reappear on a different network. The use of state or user credentials rather than network IDs is important here. A user may access via several devices and networks and obtain multiple accounts. The ease with which a user can obtain access is an important usability issue here. Multiple accounts can be useful for separating concerns, or abused to discard bad records of behaviour or provide false credentials between identities (a "Sybil" attack).

Devices which do not have traditional user input devices create a problem for providing credentials. Various techniques have been explored to verify co-location with another device [15]. This might provide access to a local service, or allow the second device to act as input or bridge where a more distant service must be accessed. Similarly, service access might be restricted to users who connect through the right network.

4.2.6 Adaptive Communications

We now move further up the protocol stack to consider transport and application issues. When considering the mobility, device variation and network variation inherent in pervasive computing we identify several issues: (quoting from [3])

- Adaptability to large-grained system resource variation.
- Adaptation ... with regard to overhead, and degree of synchrony depending on degree of connectivity.
- The definition of adaptation paths from user-level QoS parameters.
- Identifying the most suitable resources to connect to.
- Negotiating reservations and adaptations to work within limits.
- Migrating to reflect changing needs and availability.

Adaptation to context we defer to Chap. 5. In this chapter we shall consider the adaptation of communications to the network at hand.

4.2.7 Synchrony

The potential for network identity to change and appropriate servers to change due to movement, and for frequent and unpredictable disconnection leads to a need for protocols which accommodate this. In internet systems design the TCP protocol offers a stable, rate managed connection, with facilities to recover from the occasional lost packet. Where connectivity is less assured an asynchronous approach may be more appropriate. However, this has a significant impact on design:

- Transactional protocols are, in the general case, impossible. Negative acknowledgement and revocation / rollback messages cannot be guaranteed to arrive.
- Recovery from lost messages in protocols with state is complex to achieve. Management of buffers of out-of-order delivery may be required.

- Identifiers need to be established to connect a sequence of messages, possibly from different network addresses, together.
- Guarantees on synchrony, within time bounds, on systems with shared state may need to be relaxed. This can affect systems as simple as on-line / phone calendar synchronisation as well as more complex distributed databases.

A common approach to tackling these challenges is to use a middleware bus, typically with publish-subscribe semantics. The middleware has a store and forward behaviour, allowing sender and eventual receivers to connect asynchronously. Indeed, the loose coupling may extend to senders and receivers not knowing each others identity. Subscriptions typically take the form of topic categories, where all content is categorised by the publisher, or matching of content values or attributes according to rules specified by the subscriber. Later when we consider context data, you may wish to consider the benefits of this approach to providing this information as an infrastructure service. The interested reader may find [2] a useful starting point for exploring such systems.

4.3 Names and Addresses

As ever identifiers for interfaces / devices / services exist at each layer in the protocol stack. We shall now give an overview of approaches to the problem of naming and discovery which take account of the mobility and scalability implied by many devices coming and going in pervasive computing.

4.3.1 Identifiers

We start with an overview of issues in designing identifiers. *Names* identify objects in the network: ports, devices, services etc.; while *addresses* provide not only an identifier but the information required to find it. In many networks, such as IP, the two are combined. Various forms of name exist:

- MAC addresses, uniquely identifying a port on the network but useful only over a single local network, often either hard-coded or negotiated with neighbours so requiring little infrastructure. The Ethernet MAC address provides a globally unique identifier, while some ad-hoc networks negotiate locally unique identifiers for a neighbourhood.
- Network device addresses, uniquely identifying a node on the network, useful over a wider area and so requiring greater support to ensure uniqueness. The Internet IP address is a globally unique identifier, while on a private network the IP address is simply network-unique.
- Network identifiers, identifying not a device but a network.
- Service identifier, identifying not a device but a service. The service will have an association with a device, but this may not be permanent and there may be multiple services running on a device.

- Human level names, providing a user-friendly means of identifying a resource but requiring translation into other addresses for system use and infrastructure to manage the association of names and addresses.

Where names are simply locally- or network-unique but devices can communicate then some other address is required over the wider communication, typically provided by a gateway, e.g. network address translation (NAT). Depending on the sensitivity to network bandwidth overhead and energy use the size of an address may be limited: most packets will have at least one and often both of a sender and receiver address. There is a balance to be struck here between the number of identifiers needed in a scope, the complexity of ensuring uniqueness and the overhead of a large identifier. A central assignment is conceptually simpler, but less appropriate in sensor networks and other situations where identifying, communicating with and trusting reliable central authorities is not easy to arrange. In these situations a distributed assignment of local identifiers, random identifier generation, or the use of some other more portable scheme becomes more usual.

4.3.2 Portable Addresses

As well as being able to gain a new identifier to relate to the current local network, it is sometimes useful to arrange seamless coverage over a wide geographic area. Handing over ongoing connections with new identifiers is complex. A device cannot rely on having notice that network coverage using the current identifier will cease to be available. There are two classes of solution to this problem:

- Use a WAN, such as a mobile telephone network, to achieve wider area coverage. A cellular WAN will perform its own internal handover of connections, using overlapping cells and careful service engineering.
- Use a portable identifier, which can be dynamically associated with a temporary address, while providing support for continuity. Mobile IP is an example of such a service.

The mobile IP protocol is presented in [16, 18]. It provides a means for internet devices to maintain contact with other nodes using their "home" IP address when connected to another network. As observed in [17] the technique may be applicable to ad-hoc networks with internet gateways and networks which are mobile, with their own mobile router, as well as for individual devices which are mobile. IPv6 provides some simplifications of the protocol, but we shall summarise the IPv4 version here as this is generally applicable. We shall outline the mobile IP approach below, based on these papers and the standard, but leave the detail of implementation, packet structure and security for the interested reader to take from the source.

A typical internet connection involves several important steps, which ideally will not be broken by support for mobility:

- A *mobile node* has an IP address with a *home network* which, if it provides services, may be associated with a Domain Name Service (DNS) name.

- Another device which wishes to communicate with this device can look up this name, obtain an IP address and cache this address for ongoing use.
- A packet addressed to the mobile node is routed based on its destination address. Responses are routed based on their destination address. There is not generally any other control over routes, or requirement that the two paths are the same, although the network may change routes to reflect congestion etc.
- Applications at both end points in communications should not need to be aware of the mobility. Only the mobile node should do anything different to a normal IP connection (although breaking this allows some optimisation of routing).

This last point illustrates *transparency*, which is an important concept in distributed systems. Where possible lower levels of the stack must insulate higher levels from variation, e.g. whether a file-system is local or network mounted, whether a process is local or remote, whether a connection is over fibre-optic, twisted-pair, wireless or dial-up; and whether a node is in its home network or away. As discussed in Sect. 1.3.4 transparency may break down with the range of variation in pervasive computing, but this does not mean that where it can be achieved we should not. To maintain these properties the roaming connection must therefore happen in a manner which is transparent to applications, as they cannot all be expected to re-implement systems to cope with mobility, and the domain name system, which cannot be up-dated quickly enough to support seamless mobility in realistic scenarios nor can it update cached resolutions to an old address.

Mobile IP is the result of three cooperating subsystems [18]:

1. A discovery mechanism, which allows devices to gain a local IP address when they connect to a *foreign network*. DHCP alone is not sufficient as this implies a change of identity at the client which typically requires restarting services.
2. A *home agent*, which this new address can be registered with.
3. A mechanism to deliver data addressed to its home network identity to its temporary foreign address. This may make use of a *foreign agent* in IPv4. A service discovery protocol (see Sect. 4.3.3) will be needed for the mobile node to identify a suitable foreign agent.

The mobile IP protocol operates as follows, and illustrated in Fig. 4.3:

1. The mobile node has a long term home IP address.
2. The mobile node discovers a foreign agent and registers with it, or is able to obtain a foreign address and perform this function itself. The address of this end-point is the *care-of* address. The foreign-agent will be provided with a data link address, which is portable between networks.
3. The mobile node registers this care-of address with its home agent, which also becomes the end-point for the home IP address.
4. Another *correspondent* node wishing to communicate with the mobile node sends to its home IP address as usual.
5. The home agent acts as a proxy for the mobile node, forms a tunnel, forwarding the packets received encapsulated in packets addressed to the care-of address.
6. The foreign agent, if present, forwards these packets to the mobile node.

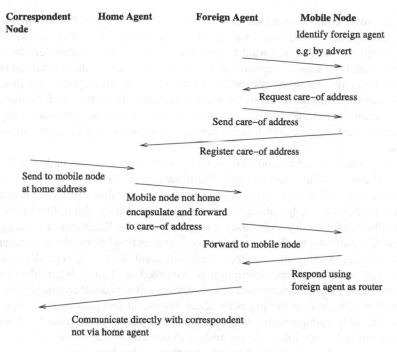

Fig. 4.3 An illustration of the main interactions in mobile IP, based on [18]

7. The mobile node processes the packets as usual and response packets can be routed in the usual way, without use of mobile IP. The foreign-agent typically acts as the gateway router, forming a routing triangle of home agent–correspondent node–foreign agent.

8. When moving network again the previous foreign agent may be informed of the new care-of address, in order to allow forwarding of datagrams and so minimise loss. This is known as *smooth handover*.

4.3.3 Discovery

In an internet situation *naming* of resources is common: one tends to use the same services over and over, e.g. mail server, printer, web site etc. Naming serves two important functions here: it provides a human identifier for configuration and it provides indirection between the service required and the port providing it. The redirection allows reconfiguration of the underlying hardware for a service with which users want a long-term association. The redirection service is typically provided by DNS, possibly supported by local protocols such as NIS. These require local knowledge and configuration for forming a connection to the proper name resolution system.

In pervasive computing the scenario is somewhat different [5]. A user will wish to move through the world, forming very temporary connections with many services. The system and user do not want to find and manually enter parameters for each such service, they want the environment to configure itself to their needs. In order to ease the configuration of systems a discovery system must support the description of services and the necessary protocols. The description may include features, API, location and availability etc., allowing systems to choose amongst a range of services to best support fault-tolerant service provision which matches the users' needs.

The volume of potential connections makes user entry of names undesirable, and the provision of unique names hard. The diversity of networks in any one place makes identifying an authoritative local-network based discovery system harder, as this implies knowledge about local configurations and a single local network. Where the network connection uses a protocol such as Bluetooth any supported discovery is naturally local; where the network connection has a wider area coverage additional mechanisms are required to support local discovery, typically using a location identifier and scope description as discussed in Chap. 7. Where the desired connection is not with some infrastructure service, but with another transient device, notifications rather than polling become an important mechanism for scalability. The overhead of managed directories, such as DNS, becomes too great for dynamic services and allowing updates to be pushed to devices on the arrival or (managed) departure of another device becomes an attractive mode of interaction that DNS and DHCP do not support. Where departures are not well managed (and this has to be expected in pervasive computing, due to power and mobility) a mechanism such as expiry of adverts is required, to avoid the name / service space becoming clogged with out of date data.

In the absence of a name alternative resource identification methods are required. A resource *description* allows search for- and/or registration for notifications about local services by type, with no human naming required. Alternatively a user may be able to identify the physical representation of the service, and request association using some identifier. This might be as simple as a QR code or RFID tag, or requiring some more complex evidence that the pair are co-located, typically to provide security through physical rather than technological constraints. A selection of such systems are described in [15], and the choice of appropriate evidence discussed.

4.4 Models of Resource

We mentioned the large variation in available resources above. The scale of the variations expected in pervasive computing cannot be hidden from users, but must be adapted to. With ever increasing concerns about energy consumption, adaptation of power consumption may become a more mainstream topic and some of these issues revisited outside pervasive computing. Adaptation requires an understanding of the constraints to be met. Where the system constrains interaction this implies resource management.

There are several aspects to effective resource management, including:

- Identify resources and the units of consumption.
- Identify whether the resource is renewed over time, e.g. network bandwidth, or consumed over time, e.g. battery power (ignoring recharging).
- Identify the availability of the resource. Inputs to this process include design specifications and monitoring for prediction of actual availability.
- Managing reservations against future availability, where expected use can be predicted, e.g. for downloading a large file.
- Performing admission control using the model of availability and reservation. A negotiation process may be part of this, where shortfall is given to allow adjustments or seniority claimed by the requester causing previous reservations to be adjusted and adapted to.
- Monitoring and managing the actual consumption against admitted requests and actual availability. For some resources it may be possible to control use, for others misuse of a reservation may lead to future sanctions. Adaptation and renegotiation of reservations may be required where actual availability do not meet expectations.
- Notification of resource levels to applications. Where a complex admission control system is not possible a simple state based adaptation of behaviour may be offered, as seen in laptop power management.
- Reconfiguration of systems as resource availability changes. As resources run low or new resources become available systems may reconfigure to direct consumption elsewhere for best performance (at a local or system level of the measure). This may include migration of services to nodes with greater resources where the service is not already available.

The idea of resource reservation is not new: networks and mainframes have been considering this for many years. Adapting these techniques to more autonomous, more distributed and more transient relationships is a challenge. The most significant use in practical pervasive systems is adapting to power states and considering consumption in design. Apart from these approaches the techniques described later for monitoring and adapting to context can be applied to the adaptation of systems to resource fluctuations.

4.5 Standards

We conclude this chapter with a brief categorisation of three currently important standards for wireless networks for PAN and LAN communication. The discussion in this section draws from the standards, product data sheets and survey papers, including [7, 14].

4.5.1 WiFi—IEEE 802.11

The IEEE 802.11 family of standards had its first member approved in 1997. These standards define the physical layer and associated medium access and hand-off. The architecture of the network is formed around the basic service set (BSS), which replicates much of the model of LANs.

There are several sub-standards within 802.11, providing variations on a theme. 802.11a uses a 5 GHz ISM band, is not widely used today, and is incompatible with many other versions of the standard. 802.11b, and the other variants we shall consider here use the 2.4 GHz ISM band, with up to 14 (depending on location) channels—although these overlap. This version was used in many consumer products and is still widely supported by more modern devices as it is compatible with newer versions of the standard. 802.11b uses Direct Sequence Spread Spectrum (DHSS) modulation and has a maximum data rate of 11 Mb/s; 802.11g uses orthogonal frequency division multiplexing (OFDM) to achieve a 54 Mb/s data rate over a range of up to 100 m. All of these versions use the same CSMA/CA MAC protocol.

The power output of IEEE 802.11 is generally between 30 mW and 100 mW, although this varies with the various sub-standards, chip sets and antennae. In [14] the power consumption was found to be 709 mW (receive) to 722 mW (transmit), and 13 mJ/Mb. We shall refer to these figures in the two subsections below as well. Note that they depend on particular chip sets, and that different patterns of low-power mode (if any) / listen / receive / transmit with different traffic patterns will give different results. The normalised power consumption figure of mJ/Mb is the important comparison if high throughput is required, while the absolute power consumption is more important if the network handles less data volume or speed, but energy budgets are tight.

In [7] the spatial capacity of 802.11g is estimated at up to 400 kb/s/m^2, if the highest data rate is achieved. The spatial capacity results from a maximum of four co-existing basic service sets each covering up to 100 m^2. In interpreting this figure the long range, large number of devices (2007) which can belong to each BSS and that each may have a data rate of 54 Mb/s and so achieve good throughput when needed must be considered. In applications where all stations require a high throughput all the time the random access model of wireless LANs is not so strong as contention starts to degrade this performance.

4.5.2 Bluetooth—IEEE 802.15.1

Bluetooth is a proprietary standard, first released in 1998, evolving from earlier work by Ericsson and including Nokia, IBM, Intel and Toshiba at first and many other companies over time. The IEEE 802.15.1 standard derived from Bluetooth in 2002, but developments in Bluetooth continue[1].

---

[1] http://www.bluetooth.com/ and http://www.bluetooth.org/.

The standard defines both the physical and data link layers of the stack, with connection oriented or connection less services. Higher level services including a serial emulation (RFCOMM) and service discovery (SDP) are also provided and IP and higher level protocols may be run over a Bluetooth connection. Audio transmissions at 64 kb/s run outside the data communications in the protocol stack and operate as a point-to-point link between master and a slave. Most data communications operate as a connection less broadcast from master to one or all slaves, with addressing authorising a response in the next time slot.

The main unit of organisation in Bluetooth is the *piconet*. Piconets have a master station and up to 7 active slave stations sharing a single radio channel. Slaves are paired with the master by responding to a new device inquiry from the master with its address. A piconet can support up to 1 Mb/s data rate, with three audio channels of 64 kb/s or one data channel of 723 kb/s or of 433 kb/s two-way.

Bluetooth has narrower bands than 802.11 and shorter range, so greater density of communications. The radio interface (the usual mode) uses the 2.4 GHz band, with 79 channels at 1 MHz spacing operated in a frequency hopping spread spectrum (FHSS) sequence. This avoids ongoing interference in any one channel, and the sequence used is defined by the master and so sustained interference with other piconets is avoided as any use of the same channel at the same time is transient.

The range is up to approximately 10 m around the master station (although some higher power devices are available). In order to achieve this, the power output of Bluetooth is generally between 1 mW and 100 mW. In [14] the power consumption was found to be 84 mW (receive) to 103 mW (transmit), and 116 to 143 mJ/Mb.

In [7] the spatial capacity of Bluetooth is estimated at up to 25 kb/s/m^2, this capacity benefits from the ability to run many (20) piconets with a limited range, but each with a limited number of devices. Piconets can be interconnected, by nodes which are active in more than one piconet, although not as a master in more than one.

4.5.3 ZigBee—IEEE 802.15.4

The ZigBee alliance[2] was formed in 2002 and released a specification in 2005, which is based on the 2003 version of IEEE 802.15.4. IEEE 802.15.4 defines the data link layer, in particular MAC protocols, while ZigBee adds network layer and security functions over this.

IEEE 802.15.4 is another PAN standard, with design goals of long battery life, simple cheap components, and accepting lower throughput than Bluetooth, up to 250 kb/s over a range of 10 to 100 m. These properties make it ideal for sensor networks, smart tags, toys etc. There are three classes of node: coordinator, router and end device, reflecting support for multi-hop, not just simple cell topologies. The topology can be arranged as a star with a central coordinator and low-latency

---

[2]http://www.zigbee.org.

communications with end devices; or as a network of peers where nodes route for each other. Nodes have two modes: *CSMA/CA* with nodes always on, and *beacon-enabled* where nodes sleep between a variable beacon interval.

IEEE 802.15.4 uses either the 2.4 GHz or 868/915 MHz (depending on country) bands, with 16 channels at 5 MHz spacing or 1/10 channels of 0.6/2 MHz spacing respectively. The power output of ZigBee is generally between 1 mW and 100 mW. To some extent this is determined by licensing and what is needed to provide the stated range with usual antenna designs, hence the similarity with Bluetooth. In [14] the power consumption was found to be 81 mW (receive) to 74 mW (transmit), and 324 to 296 mJ/Mb.

The MAC protocol is CSMA/CA based, although simpler than IEEE 802.11, where the peer-to-peer arrangement is used, or a fixed-time slotted access model with some use of CSMA/CA for slot negotiation in a star topology. The star topology also supports some guaranteed time slots, which together with the fixed-time arrangement enable quality of service guarantees. Compared to the other standards discussed the maximum number of cell nodes, in excess of 65,000, is significantly higher. We estimate the spatial capacity to be 12 kb/s/m^2, but an experimental figure has proved hard to find in the literature. Although this figure is lower than the other networks, the moderate power consumption and provision for multi-hop networks and a high number of nodes that can form a cell make it ideal for many ad-hoc and sensor network applications.

4.6 Summary

In this chapter we have provided a brief survey of networking issues arising in pervasive computing and some of the standards and solutions that have found success in the past. We see that mobility, error, variation and efficient use of resources (power, spatial bandwidth etc.) are key drivers. Proper selection of protocols for the system needs; efficient design; and provision of software designed to adapt to change and recover from error and disconnection are important tools responding to these challenges. Connectivity is one example of a wider sort of variation, called context which is an important consideration in pervasive computing. This is the subject of a large portion of the book—but it should be remembered that network conditions are part of context (and can be substituted for physical context in many lab classes if necessary) and that the tools we introduced here may be applied in the wider treatment of context as you read on. The topics here also form the foundation for Chap. 9 on sensor networking.

4.7 Suggested Readings

- An article surveying the implications of various issues on UbiComp. It stands as a system software introduction, but is better read in the context of the hardware and networks chapters rather than in the introduction. Tim Kindberg and

Armando Fox. System software for ubiquitous computing. *IEEE Pervasive Computing*, 1:70–81, January 2002

- A survey paper on QoS implications of mobility Dan Chalmers and Morris Sloman. A survey of quality of service in mobile computing environments. *IEEE Communications Surveys*, 2nd Quarter 1999, 1999
- A discussion of sensor network platforms Jason Hill, Mike Horton, Ralph Kling, and Lakshman Krishnamurthy. The platforms enabling wireless sensor networks. *Commun. ACM*, 47:41–46, June 2004
- A discussion of power management and resource planning, including network issues, in sensor network design Pei Zhang, Christopher M. Sadler, Stephen A. Lyon, and Margaret Martonosi. Hardware design experiences in zebranet. In *Proceedings of the 2nd international conference on Embedded networked sensor systems*, SenSys '04, pages 227–238, New York, NY, USA, 2004. ACM
- A study of energy use in networks Laura Marie Feeney and Martin Nilsson. Investigating the energy consumption of a wireless network interface in an ad hoc networking environment. In *INFOCOM*, pages 1548–1557, 2001.
- A quite substantial paper addressing programming issues raised in this chapter, including adaptation, migration and asynchronous communications Robert Grimm, Janet Davis, Eric Lemar, Adam Macbeth, Steven Swanson, Thomas Anderson, Brian Bershad, Gaetano Borriello, Steven Gribble, and David Wetherall. System support for pervasive applications. *ACM Trans. Comput. Syst.*, 22:421–486, November 2004
- A survey of discovery systems. W. Keith Edwards. Discovery systems in ubiquitous computing. *IEEE Pervasive Computing*, 5:70–77, 2006
- A view on the state of Mobile IP, including an update on the classic 1997 paper [18]. As with many papers which predict the future or comment on works in progress it would be interesting for the student to follow up the loose ends and see where we have got to. Charles E. Perkins. Mobile IP. *IEEE Communications Magazine*, 40(5):66–82, 2002
- A useful introduction to the design and simulated analysis of the performance of IEEE 802.15.4 is given in Jianliang Zheng and Myung J. Lee. *A comprehensive performance study of IEEE 802.15.4*, Chap. 4, page 14. IEEE Press, Wiley Interscience, 2003
- Further textbook reading on networks giving more detail but remaining general can be found in e.g. [1, 4, 12, 19].

4.8 Laboratory Exercises: Network Measurement

Survey various networks and find, through experiment, their delay and throughput. Remember that both delay and throughput matter for application performance—although the importance of each depends on the application. A simple version of this can be written using ping. The next step would be to include application, e.g. web server, performance in the measurements.

The real exercise here is in systematically collecting data and presenting it:

1. Identify a range of devices with different first-hop networks. Collect measurements from these. Collect several measurements, say 20 from each. If possible, note any driver reported bandwidth / negotiated rate, signal-to-noise ratio etc. In the case of wireless networks it would be interesting to find different situations with different conditions.
2. The variable first-hop, probably including wireless networks, will be a significant limiting factor in communications. However, it would be useful to understand what its effect is separate to the whole system effect. Consider whether you can collect measurements which exclude the first-hop, or at least as many of the later hops as possible. Consider whether you can collect measurements to a different end-point which change as much of the later hops as possible.
3. Next, consider whether the payload data, both sent and received, has a significant effect. Re-run the test with a different payload.
4. Finally, consider whether there are external effects in play. The most obvious effect is from additional traffic: both at the end-point and locally. If you have access to the management of these systems the traffic level may be visible to you. If you do not, then re-testing at different times is a reasonable strategy. In addition, running two tests in parallel from different devices may indicate any marginal effect of an additional measurement.
5. Finally, plot the collected data on a graph. A box and whisker plot against each condition is probably the most appropriate form.

4.9 Laboratory Exercises: Sensitivity and Noise in Signals

This lab is designed to combine your knowledge of sensors with ideas of wireless communications. The aim is to communicate by flashing lights, e.g. by Morse code.

1. Consider the definition of Morse code, e.g. [10]. Write a program to flash LEDs on the Phidget board in Morse code in response to an input. The code should allow for variable sending speed.
2. Write a program (or separate thread in the first program) to receive Morse code using a light sensor. It may be useful to use a 2nd light sensor to detect ambient light to help define signal thresholds, or to use as a second receiver to corroborate the received signal. Consider also the response speed of light sensors. Have this program output the received signal.
3. Manage the sending rate. Define a simple protocol which allows the two partners to negotiate an acceptable data rate based on the response of the sensors and the noise experienced. Consider also an ACK/NACK signal to allow error correction.
4. To extend this lab you might like to work with another group or use 2 Phidget kits on 2 computers. If you agree the rate / control protocol then you should be able to exchange data.
5. To extend this lab you might like to consider other signalling protocols, for data encoding and/or control signals. How does the change in protocol affect the average data rate and the overheads vs. good-put?

References

1. Adelstein, F., Gupta, S.K.S., Richard, G.G. III, Schwiebert, L.: Fundamentals of Mobile and Pervasive Computing. McGraw-Hill, New York (2004)
2. Baldoni, R., Querzoni, L., Virgillito, A.: Distributed event routing in publish/subscribe communication systems: a survey. Technical report, Universitá di Roma la Sapienza (2005)
3. Chalmers, D., Sloman, M.: A survey of quality of service in mobile computing environments. IEEE Commun. Surv. **2**, 2–10 (1999)
4. Cook, D.J., Das, S.K. (eds.): Smart Environments. Wiley, New York (2005)
5. Edwards, W.K.: Discovery systems in ubiquitous computing. IEEE Pervasive Comput. **5**, 70–77 (2006)
6. Feeney, L.M., Nilsson, M.: Investigating the energy consumption of a wireless network interface in an ad hoc networking environment. In: INFOCOM, pp. 1548–1557 (2001)
7. Ferro, E., Potorti, F.: Bluetooth and wi-fi wireless protocols: a survey and a comparison. IEEE Wirel. Commun. **12**(1), 12–26 (2005)
8. Grimm, R., Davis, J., Lemar, E., Macbeth, A., Swanson, S., Anderson, T., Bershad, B., Borriello, G., Gribble, S., Wetherall, D.: System support for pervasive applications. ACM Trans. Comput. Syst. **22**, 421–486 (2004)
9. Hill, J., Horton, M., Kling, R., Krishnamurthy, L.: The platforms enabling wireless sensor networks. Commun. ACM **47**, 41–46 (2004)
10. ITU: Recommendation—international morse code. Technical Report ITU-R M.1677, International Telecommunication Union (2004)
11. Jones, C.E., Sivalingam, K.M., Agrawal, P., Chen, J.C.: A survey of energy efficient network protocols for wireless networks. Wircl. Netw. **7**, 343–358 (2001)
12. Karl, H., Willig, A.: Protocols and Architectures for Wireless Sensor Networks. Wiley, New York (2005)
13. Kindberg, T., Fox, A.: System software for ubiquitous computing. IEEE Pervasive Comput. **1**, 70–81 (2002)
14. Lee, J.-S., Su, Y.-W., Shen, C.-C.: A comparative study of wireless protocols: bluetooth, UWB, ZigBee, and Wi-Fi. In: Industrial Electronics Society, 2007. IECON 2007. 33rd Annual Conference of the IEEE, pp. 46–51 (2007)
15. Malkani, Y.A., Chalmers, D., Wakeman, I., Dhomeja, L.D.: Towards a general system for secure device pairing by demonstration of physical proximity. In: Proceedings of 2nd International Workshop on Mobile and Wireless Networks Security (MWNS'09) (2009)
16. Perkins, C.E. (ed.): IP Mobility Support for IPv4. Technical Report RFC 3220, Network Working Group (2002)
17. Perkins, C.E.: Mobile IP. IEEE Commun. Mag. **40**(5), 66–82 (2002)
18. Perkins, C.E., Myles, A.F., Watson, T.J.: Mobile IP. IEEE Commun. Mag. **35**(5), 84–99 (1997)
19. Tanenbaum, A.: Computer Networks, 4th edn. Prentice Hall Professional Technical Reference (2002)
20. Weiser, M.: Nomadic issues in ubiquitous computing (1996)
21. Zhang, P., Sadler, C.M., Lyon, S.A., Martonosi, M.: Hardware design experiences in zebranet. In: Proceedings of the 2nd International Conference on Embedded Networked Sensor Systems, SenSys '04, pp. 227–238. ACM, New York (2004)
22. Zheng, J., Lee, M.J.: A Comprehensive Performance Study of IEEE 802.15.4. IEEE Press, Wiley Interscience, New York (2003). Chap. 4, p. 14

Part III
Sensing The World

Chapter 5
Classification and Use of Context

We have already alluded to "adapting to the context of use" in Chap. 1 several times, as it is part of the solution to many of the issues in pervasive computing. We shall now set about trying to understand this better.

5.1 Input and Output in Pervasive Computing

In a traditional computer system inputs and outputs are well-defined and have explicit behaviours associated with them. Inputs might include keyboards, mice, microphones and networks; outputs include screens, printers and networks. In an office, smart or not, the environment presents ways to interact with it and control it: doors have handles, lights have switches, heating controls have dials, chairs can be arranged in various ways and so on. Each of these either has a well-defined behaviour (handles, switches, dials) or conforms to local social norms (door left open means I'm available, chairs may be arranged differently for meetings and presentations). In a pervasive computing environment computing systems will still require interfaces: including screens and keyboards, styluses for hand-held, voice commands and so on. At the same time *context awareness* demands an awareness of the environment, changing display preferences if it is dark, changing patterns of interruption in a meeting and so on. We should take care to distinguish between inputs and outputs required to do a job and context, which should be subtler—certainly it should not be necessary to switch the lights off or on in order to get a desired behaviour!

5.2 Defining Context

The term *context* is used in many fields and is used informally. We shall restrict ourselves to a systems view of pervasive computing here, although it is necessarily

D. Chalmers, *Sensing and Systems in Pervasive Computing*,
Undergraduate Topics in Computer Science,
DOI 10.1007/978-0-85729-841-6_5, © Springer-Verlag London Limited 2011

quite a human concept. It is hoped that readers familiar with other uses of the term will find our interpretation is not a radical departure.

Context can include many different sorts of sensed information about the environment:

- Location, co-location, and related locations
- Identity, of the user, of co-located people
- Activity
- Time
- Sound levels
- Light levels
- Motion, both macro-level speed and location traces, but also micro-level patterns of acceleration, vibration and orientation
- and many more...

We shall refer to these different sorts of contextual information as *aspects*. As well as these human, visible aspects of context, arguably properties of the computing environment also have an effect on the user's interaction. These might include:

- Available network bandwidth and delay
- Available computing power, memory and storage
- Availability of particular interfaces, such as screens, speakers, microphones
- Screen size and colour depth

However we shall see that context is not defined by the aspects that are, and are not, "it"—but more by the role those aspects play. There are many similar, but varied, definitions of context:

The dictionary [27] gives a definition of "the circumstances relevant to something under consideration".

Abowd identifies "Who, what, where, when, why" as a "good minimal set of necessary context" [1].

Dey defines context as:

> ...any information that can be used to characterise the situation of an entity. An entity is a person, place, or object that is considered relevant to the interaction between a user and an application, including the user and applications themselves. [8]

However, this is qualified by a later comment that "certain types of context are ...more important than others. These are location, identity, activity and time."

Brown et al. [4] suggest that context can be used to describe "the environment, situation, state, surroundings, task and so on".

Petrelli et al. [17] discuss what context means in different fields and arrive at a definition similar to that in [8], restricting the entity to the person who is interacting with that specific application at a certain time, which seems to omit issues of multiple users in a space or remotely interacting users.

In [10] Dourish describes context as "information of middling relevance"—it is not something so central to an activity that it defines it, neither is it formed of details which have no bearing on the activity.

In Schmidt's PhD thesis [22] he compares context to senses. In this discussion, he notes that different species have senses (and development of senses) which align well to their environment and behaviour within the world. We can informally think of context as the senses which an application has developed to support its relationship with the world.

The user, the task they are trying to carry out, the application in use and the data in use often have special status but may also influence the subtler responses of context aware systems. Given the dictionary definition, if we take the thing under consideration to be some interaction with a computing device, we have a definition which encompasses the others quite satisfactorily, without relying on examples. We therefore define context as:

> Context is the circumstances relevant to the interaction between a user and their computing environment [5].

In early work, such as Cyberguide [2], the context considered was necessarily limited—they considered only location and orientation and in many other cases location is a crucial form of context or input to pervasive applications. (It should already be clear that in a navigation application "location" is *input* rather than *context*—it is a centrally important piece of data for the application.) Indeed location has been the most deeply explored aspect of context and in many cases goes well beyond "middling relevance", with highly developed sensors, processing, abstractions and uses, hence we return to location for a deeper discussion in Chap. 7 where we can properly address it without separating its role as context and input.

5.2.1 An Introduction to Some Aspects of Context

There are many potential aspects to context, which we sample briefly below (and explore in greater depth as we move on), inspired by known devices, our own work and the literature cited elsewhere, e.g. [3]. These can be classed in various ways: human factors vs. physical environment, and sub-categories of these such as personal, social, infrastructure, environmental conditions and so on [22]; by the types of processing they require; by whether the sensing infrastructure is attached to the described object or is remote from it etc.

Returning to the senses analogy [22], we note that not all applications require the same aspects of context in order to properly adapt, or the same levels of detail, much as different species evolve senses to meet their needs. In designing pervasive computing we might aspire to extend this analogy further: firstly, by providing the physical context sensing in the environment and allowing applications choose what aspects they interpret; secondly by allowing individual application instances to cope with temporary loss of some aspects of context, either with reduced transparency in responding to context or by discovering proxies for the missing data.

Location Depending on the application location may be the only form of context considered and we discuss the issues in more depth in Chap. 7. The key issues arising are:

- Is the location that of the sensor or of another party (to be tracked or to identify co-location)?
- What terms of reference (grid system, place name, relative position from observer etc.) are to be used?
- What scope (room, building, country, world) is location required over?
- What are the limits of the sensors and supporting infrastructure being used (often indoor / outdoor only)? Are multiple sources of data available?

Motion Motion can be viewed as location traces through time, but is interesting and different enough to merit its own entry here. Various techniques are available, including:

- Describing current velocity from recent location reports. This requires some trade-off between short term noise and accurate, timely reporting—topics which we tackle in more depth in Chap. 6.
- Motion sensors, such as ultrasonic and infra-red detectors and data extraction from video, which report motion within their range rather than of a located device. There will be choices to make about the scope of the detection, sensitivity and ability to describe rate of motion.
- Action detectors, where beam-breaking; turn-stiles; many different forms of operating switches (tilt, contact etc.); or triggering localised detectors, e.g. RFID, describes motion through a special "capture zone" but does not follow motion in other places. See also [16] for examples of localised presence and motion detection.
- Using accelerometers to describe orientation, direction and speed.
- Using accelerometers to describe small-scale motion, such as vibration.
- Processing patterns of sensed data, over large or small time-scales, to describe the differences between types of motion (walk, run, cycle); or to find patterns of motion in daily routines (commute, coffee break, work at desk).

There are various Phidget sensors that might be used to explore some of the differences here in the laboratory sessions. As for location there are questions to answer and trade-offs to make before selecting the right technique for an application, but there are also some generic (to many sensors and other problems) techniques to apply such as event listeners, filters and pattern detection—which we shall explore in this part of the book.

Identity of People Often we seek to know who is present. Identity badges [12], recognising Bluetooth IDs of personal devices e.g. [16], recognising voice or other bio-signatures are some possible approaches.

Sensory Environment The user's environment may affect their ability or desire to interact in various ways, e.g. ability to see a keyboard, preference for audio notifications, ability to concentrate under stress; it might also affect their preferences in applications such as environment control, e.g. heating behaviour. Sound and light are the most obvious of these environmental factors and we elaborate on these below. We might also include vibration (noted under *motion* above), humidity, air quality and other "comfort" factors.

- Sound can be used as an indicator of place and activity; without great analysis we might separate quiet, a monologue, a conversation, and music by analysing levels and patterns of level and frequency components. If we can identify quiet times then applications can understand background noise, possibly adjusting audio notifications to a suitable volume for the context or to use non-audio alerts when they are more appropriate, e.g. in a cinema or rock concert.
- Light levels are helpful to understand in order to adapt user interfaces. Light can be illuminating, making input devices visible; however it can also be interfering making computer screens hard to read or dazzling drivers. Light also serves as an indicator of activities: flickering might be a TV, spectrum indicates daylight vs. artificial light; analysis of variation over slightly longer times might indicate movement.

5.3 Categorising Uses of Context

How do we determine Dourish's "middling relevance"? Is it by the effort put into understanding it, or the subtlety of the effect, or something else? Abowd [2] notes that context works best when captured "behind the scenes". This gives an alternative approach to Dourish's middling relevance: data which matters, but not so much that the user wants to be providing it all the time if the application is to disappear into the woodwork. The other side of this approach to context is that the responses must matter, but not so much that they form the application itself. This fits with our consideration of the *circumstances relevant*—the "conditions that might affect an action" [27], rather than "conditions which define an action".

What then are the responses to context we may wish to consider? How might systems be *context-aware*? Dey defines this as:

A system is context-aware if it uses context to provide relevant information and/or services to the user, where relevancy depends on the user's task. [8]

Remember that *activity* was a form of context above, and should be treated as different to *task*: a task is a practical goal, such as making deliveries, enjoying the museum; while activity might be driving or walking.

We identify seven uses of contextual information, drawing from [4–6, 8, 21]:

1. *Context display* where sensed context is presented to the user, e.g. display of current location. Arguably, this is either primary display of information, or supporting user awareness of the system's interpretation of context to explain other behaviours.
2. *Contextual augmentation* annotates data with the context of its generation, e.g. meeting notes can be associated with attendees and location of the meeting [4]. Data must be stored so that any future indexing or searching is facilitated.
3. *Context aware configuration*, e.g., to cause printing to be on the nearest printer, or cause selection of nearby proxies when needed. The model must help answer questions such as "find the nearest", for instance when relocating a display to a screen near the user [13, 28].

4. *Context triggered actions* [21] such as automatically loading map data for the next location predicted (although this might also be seen as input rather than context); or pausing the TV when a phone rings.
5. *Contextual mediation* is the use of context to modify services provided or the data requested to best meet the needs and limits arising from the context of the interaction [5].
6. *Contextual Adaptation of the Environment* might be cast as a form of context triggered actions, but in this class of context awareness we consider an application whose behaviours are manifested in the environment (lighting, heating, media systems etc.) rather than a "computing" application which is the focus of a task.
7. *Context aware presentation* refers to the adaptation of the user interface or the presentation of data, e.g. adjusting interaction widgets according to the display device; or choosing appropriate message notifications for the context. This use of context is closely aligned to user preference management.

In the last five cases (often collected together under the heading *contextual adaptation* [8]) context data may be matched to test conditions to enable or trigger specifications, policies or actions. Context may also be used as parameters to modify these responses. For instance, we may want to trigger policies relating to being "in a car" when driving, while also changing the behaviour of a navigation system depending on how far we are from our destination. In these cases we need well typed context data which can be used to make tests such as equality, difference and order; and also to be used as function parameters. This set of possible uses lead us to a wider definition of *context-aware*:

> A system is context-aware if it uses context to enhance its behaviour to become more appropriate to the user's context.

We consider behaviour to include both visible behaviours, including those which are only visible after the fact such as contextual recall using augmentation of stored data; and systems behaviours that are only visible through side effects, such as greater speed or longer battery life.

5.4 Values into Meanings

In order to be useful to users, and their applications, raw sensor data must be given meaning. Salber, Dey and Abowd [20] identify this as a difficult problem in using context: pinning down a meaning for a given set of readings typically requires knowledge of the hardware, installation and application domain.

In [11] Gellersen, Schmidt and Beigl describe a generic architecture for processing context data: the current context, e.g. "user sleeps" is extracted from sensors reading "dark, silent, indoors, nighttime, horizontal, still", which in turn is derived from particular values in light sensors, noise sensors (integrated over time), location sensors, a clock and time-zone, and orientation and movement sensors on the

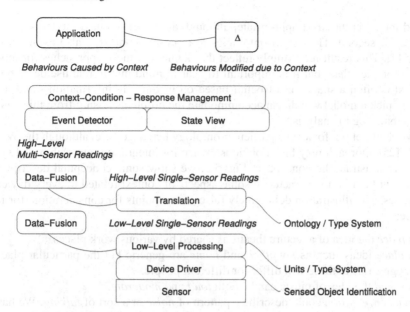

Fig. 5.1 The context stack: processing and applying sensor data for context awareness

body. Although arranged differently other researchers follow similar patterns, e.g. Dey [9] describes a system of context sensors, widgets that interpret the sensor readings, and aggregators that collect together multiple information sources about different aspects of context and/or related objects; [15] also presents a stack-based model of sensor processing arriving at application adaptation to context. This processing model of successive abstraction seems appropriate, allowing flexible organisation from reusable components and separation of the different problems in deriving meaning from sensors in the world. The *context stack* is illustrated in Fig. 5.1.

In our stack model data are collected from sensors via some device driver (this is provided in the Phidgets library). Some low level processing may be made, normalising the data, adjusting for known sensor properties, transforming raw values to a scale with units etc. (the Phidgets libraries perform some of these functions). For sensors providing more complex data, e.g. time series readings from vibration sensors, accelerometers or microphones, the low-level data may be more complex, e.g. peak and RMS readings for certain frequency bands, but still essentially rooted in sensor-level data.

The low-level data will usually need to be transformed into higher-level meaning. Applications should have responses to context which connect a human understanding of the world around them into useful behaviours. In many cases this will require assigning human-understandable meaning to the sensed data, although in some systems-level adaptation low-level values may remain appropriate.

Once processed into meaning context needs a representation which applications can work with. Strang and Linhoff-Popien discuss the relative merits of different approaches to representing context in [26]. Their conclusion is that an ontology based model is the most appropriate, although an object oriented model seems to be a close second. The use of ontologies to represent context is also explored by Chen [7]. This result may simply reflect the richness of these approaches for modelling complex data, but it is important to bear in mind that in real use describing context is often a statement of belief based on incomplete information—and it is wise to pick a model which can accommodate the problems arising from this while also submitting to analysis.

We shall not put forward a particular ontology language here, although the W3C OWL [25] approach may be an obvious choice for integration into web based systems. To illustrate the concept, in Fig. 5.2, we show some conceptual descriptors that might be used to characterise some aspects of context related to every day experiences. The illustration deliberately raises some points for consideration, for instance:

- In *place* the idea of a lecture theatre is shared by various work places.
- In *place* ideas such as *my office* and *home* are generic but the particular places that give rise to these will differ for different people.
- In *sound* the idea of music can be both *loud* and *moderate*.
- That *conversation* could describe a pattern of *noise* or a sort of *talking*. We have represented these as the same concept—if the labels should refer to different concepts then either different names should be used or the place in the tree described.
- In *light* we have collected together both type and level, but really these are two dimensions to describe light much as level and content can describe noise.
- In *light* and *sound* the discrete conditions such as *bright* and *dim* sit on a continuum. How many conditions are needed and how personal are the definitions?

Which values in the ontology might describe a lecture—from the student's point of view and the lecturer's? As you explore this book you might like to refine this model and consider how these situations might be identified at lower levels in the context stack and used in higher levels.

There are many approaches to modelling context which you may wish to read about, including [7, 15, 19, 23]. We shall not expand on the detail of all of these here, but suggest a single model for consideration. You may not find that this suits your purposes, and we encourage the reader to consider extending or adapting this model and examining the alternatives if this description becomes a limitation.

We use the notation $\mathscr{C}_{a,o}$ to denote a value of context for aspect, a, describing an actor or object o. The types of a value can be numerical ($\mathbb{N}$) or a node in a hierarchy of concepts (ontology) ($\mathbb{T}$). We leave the typing of aspect names and actor / object identifiers open for now, but separate ontologies may well be appropriate. The overall context for an object is

$$\mathbf{C}_o = \bigcup_{\forall a} \mathscr{C}_{a,o} \qquad (5.1)$$

Note that other meta-data may extend this model, in particular a description of the accuracy of the data will be considered later. Treating low-level and high level context data as essentially similar is convenient where we do not want to make significant interpretations, or wish to re-interpret high-level data, or wish to fuse low and

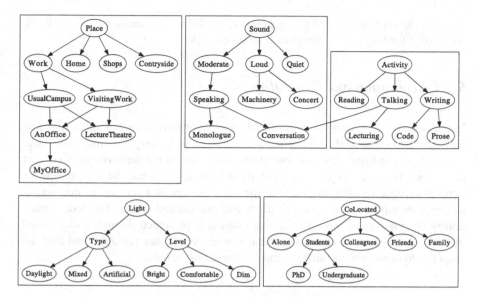

Fig. 5.2   An example ontology: describing an academic's context

high level data together for some reason. This very general notation can also be used without implying a particular implementation approach.

The object being described may have further properties: identity, e.g. "Dan", "Dan's phone" and relationships with other objects e.g. "owned-by", "friends-with". Devices will be a particularly common sort of object in such a description, not least because it is there that programs run and that sensor data is connected—indeed they often stand as proxies for people. Networked devices will have an additional relationship description, for the network path between them. The quality and cost of use of a network will often form part of the system context. An example capturing these relationships can be found in Henricksen's model [14].

This model of context describing objects allows us to examine relations between objects, e.g. knowing object location allows us to describe a person as "near" a screen and "within" a room. The relationships that can be described are simply a matter of describing comparisons between context, rather than being first-class notions which require their own language.

We should be cautious of expecting particular sensors to be available or of requiring very specific training data. The diversity of the available hardware in pervasive computing has already been highlighted as a challenge. Variation, in individual sensors, in deployments, and in presence of sensors of particular aspects of context has to be assumed in any scenario considering mobility (and where everything is static the problem of context awareness is vastly reduced but also unrealistic). Given that people move about, visit new locations, and change their behaviour over various time-scales training data (as an installation activity in particular) will become fragile over time. We tackle the issue of error and uncertainty in depth in Chap. 6. For now, we should bear in mind that generality, flexibility and learning from feedback are needed for long-term deployments to succeed [9].

5.4.1 Separation and Generality

In many research prototypes the available set of contexts is known and limited by hardware and time, while the application deployment is limited in time and space. Under these conditions it is possible to undertake a minimal deployment of context awareness. However, to properly implement context awareness we should aim for general purpose sensing, available in the environment as a service. In this way it becomes possible to separate applications and context and achieve the desired scalability [9]. Of course, this requires that context is presented through a distributed middle-ware; that the meanings associated with context are reusable; and that the response to context is encoded in terms of these abstractions.

5.5 Defining Responses to Context

Given our seven classes of context-awareness in Sect. 5.3 we should consider how we move from collecting context data to making those behaviours possible.

Context-aware configuration, -adaptation of the environment and *-triggered actions* are naturally *event* driven behaviours. When a change in context is detected, actions or reconfiguration of the system are triggered.

Contextual augmentation, -mediation and *-presentation* are interpretations of other actions, either context-triggered or user-triggered. In each case the context could be identified either by discovering the context when there is data to store, actions to mediate or data to present; or by examining an existing model of the current context. In both cases we are interested in the current *state* of the context; although the collection may be driven by polling or "new data" events (the choice depending on the efficiency of either scenario).

Context display requires that the data are collected in a structured manner, that current and past readings can be differentiated, and that we have a means of presentation. Depending on the application we may be interested in a constant presentation of *state*, or alerting the user to *events*. The mapping of state to display could be realised by a model—view pattern, by style-sheets in the manner of XML, etc. The mapping of events to display may be structured as subscription—notification etc.

The *widget* model [9, 20] for abstracting context awareness provides both a query and a call-back mechanism, supporting both of these patterns; as does the Phidget API.

The mapping of states or events to action is the activity which is described in the "context-condition—response-management" box in Fig. 5.1. While the actual responses will depend on the application, user and deployment there can be a generic architecture for describing the responses in most cases.

In our notation, we define a specification as:

$$S \rightarrow \{\text{preferences and actions}\}$$

$$\text{where } S = \bigcup \mathscr{S}_{a,o} \text{ to be matched against } C_o \qquad (5.2)$$

5.5.1 Event-Driven Behaviours

In programming event-driven behaviours are often implemented using a *listener* interface. Here an API call to the event producer registers an interest in a certain class of events, for instance a certain degree of change in some context aspect. The event generator then calls the registered listeners so that they may *consume* the event. Various formulations of this basic pattern can be found, e.g. using messaging middleware such as Elvin[1], in tuple-spaces, etc. The underlying event generation may be a result of state monitoring and comparing with event triggers in software (in which case see also the discussion of state-driven behaviours below) or may arise from hardware interrupts.

By implementing the response to events directly in the application code it becomes hard to vary the response, to reuse behaviours and to separate the response to context (and the deployed context-sensing infrastructure) from the application. An approach which supports separation of concerns is more appropriate.

Policies are commonly formulated as event–condition–action rules in systems management [24]. Here a trigger event on a certain subject can map to a policy response; the policy is checked against conditions (system state) and if the conditions are satisfied then an action is caused to take place. The action is generally described as a code fragment, which might cause a reconfiguration, or make some application call. In the example in Listing 5.1 a location change event is caught. The scale of the event is limited to at least room-level changes. The limit is written as a `delta` filter on the event, but may in fact be used to configure the event system. Next conditions are checked, confirming that the user is at work (and so wants phone calls re-routed) but not in a meeting which should not be disturbed. Finally, if the event occurs under the given conditions the code block is executed. In this case the extension of the located user is forwarded to the extension found in the directory for that location. Note that in addition to location as a trigger for the event, task, location and activity are used as state conditions in the where clause; and location is used as a function parameter in the action clause.

5.5.2 State-Driven Behaviours

State-driven behaviours may be a continuous behaviour (as in context-display) or applied on some application event. Obtaining context data will have a cost: in pro-

---

[1] http://elvin.org/.

```
on event (location) {
   delta location.place >= room
}
where {
   task within work,
   location within office,
   activity not within meeting
}
do {
   Phone.forward(Dir.getExtension(location.user),
                 Dir.getPhone(location.place))
}
```

Listing 5.1 A context event policy

cessing and in energy, arising from running the sensor and performing that processing. If context state is obtained unnecessarily often then computing power and energy are wasted, which may affect the responsiveness of other software or the lifetime of the sensor hardware. If obtaining context state is complex and only performed on request then there may be a noticeable delay introduced into interactions. State-based context awareness therefore requires a trade-off between the timeliness of the data and the effort required to process it. Where polling is an underlying mechanism for an event-based system then polling frequency may depend on predictions of when an event-worthy degree of state change may occur; similarly where state is being used to affect other behaviours the encoding of behaviour change may be used to affect this trade-off. In other cases a continuous display of accurate data may be required, or context may be used as input to a continuous function (e.g. distance from some other object) making boundary detection impossible.

Once the state has been obtained, there are various encodings of response to state available to the programmer. Logic models [18], systems of state-based specifications [6] and aspect-oriented programming all have their place. In each case a similar separation of context-driven behaviour from application-behaviour is desired to that found in the application of policies to events above.

The following example, from [6], illustrates specifications to adapt data selected in contextual mediation:

A predicted change in location causes a new map to be loaded. The context is then used to adjust the map which is loaded, for instance: if the user is travelling slowly near their destination the desired map will be small scale, showing high detail and will refresh more frequently; if the user is further from their destination on a main road the map will have a larger scale, showing less detail of small features in order to show a longer term view for faster travel. The selection of extra features, such as shops, restaurants etc. may depend on whether the journey is for work or leisure, acceptable delay and level of detail allowed on the screen etc.

An example of the maps generated by these possibilities is shown in Table 5.1. In this we see three example mediations where four aspects of context give rise to goals (the real goals are more detailed than this illustration). Aspects of context

Table 5.1 Contextual mediation of maps—an example journey from [6]. Mediation resource limits 3.6 kB/s network, 400*400 pixel screen. Dan Chalmers, Naranker Dulay, and Morris Sloman. A framework for contextual mediation in mobile and ubiquitous computing. *Personal and Ubiquitous Computing*, 8(1):1–18, 2004. http://dx.doi.org/10.1007/s00779-003-0255-6 ©2004 Springer Verlag. Reprinted by permission

Context	Adaptation Goals	Mediated Maps	Un-Mediated Maps
$9km^2$ map, 30mph, in car, for work	detail 2.2, deadline 25s, pref. major roads, pref. central detail	took 16.9s	took 46.3s
$4km^2$ map, 20mph, in car, for work	detail 2.5, deadline 30s, pref. major roads, pref. central detail	took 23.4s	took 31.7s
$4km^2$ map, 10mph, in car, for work	detail 2.5, deadline 30s, pref. all roads, pref. central detail	took 21.9s	took 26.0s

may give rise to goals on their own or in combination with other aspects. Conflict resolution algorithms are required to combine these goals into a single unambiguous behaviour specification. In each case we see an example mediated and un-mediated map, and find that the mediated maps adjust the detail to the situation and work to download deadlines; while the un-mediated maps are sometimes cluttered and take an unpredictable time to download. In the mediated case this success is despite the overhead of retrieving meta data which describes the properties of data available, including: feature types, scale, data size and bounding box. Other adaptations, such as task affecting classes of feature, also occur.

5.6 Summary

In this chapter we have started to consider in detail what context is. We have identified definitions for context, aspects of context and context-awareness—and six classes of this awareness. We have outlined the need to separate, both in hardware and code, context sensing from applications and users' interface devices. We have considered a stack model of sensor processing to arrive at context awareness, which includes common device drivers, processing of data, sensor fusion, data models and different modes of responding to context, despite the potential for variation in available sensors. The issue of meaning in context is highlighted as important, and the need for well-understood descriptions is clear—although the necessary meaning for these descriptions is often application dependent.

In the next chapters we will examine *location* as a special aspect of context, as it has the most well developed treatment; and we will consider error and uncertainty in context, as this is a large problem on its own, and we will examine the processing of sensor data in more detail.

5.7 Suggested Readings

The following readings combine models of context with applications.

- Andy Harter, Andy Hopper, Pete Steggles, Andy Ward, and Paul Webster. The anatomy of a context-aware application. *Wireless Networks*, 8(2–3):187–197, 2002
- Peter J. Brown, John D. Bovey, and Xian Chen. Context-aware applications: from the laboratory to the marketplace. *IEEE Personal Communications*, 4(5):58–64, 1997
- Either Hans W. Gellersen, Albercht Schmidt, and Michael Beigl. Multi-sensor context-awareness in mobile devices and smart artifacts. *Mob. Netw. Appl.*, 7(5):341–351, 2002

or Albrecht Schmidt, Kofi A. Aidoo, Antii Takaluoma, Urpo Tuomela, Kristoph van Laerhoven, and Walter van de Velde. Advanced interaction in context. In *1st Intl. Symposium on Handheld and Ubiquitous Computing (HUC)*, Karlsruhe, Germany, 1999

- Thomas Strang and Claudia Linnhoff-Popien. A context modeling survey. In *Workshop on Advanced Context Modelling, Reasoning And Management at Ubi-Comp*, 2004
- Karen Henricksen and Jadwiga Indulska. A software engineering framework for context-aware pervasive computing. In *PerCom*, pages 77–86. IEEE Computer Society, 2004

5.8 Laboratory Exercises: Consider Sensor Properties

The purpose of this lab is to explore the different properties of different sensors. How do they react to a change in stimulus? How consistent are these responses?

1. You should have a Phidgets kit including two to four sensors, such as: light, force, magnetic, vibration, temperature, IR reflective, touch and IR motion. A light sensor is a good idea as with LEDs a controlled stimulus can be provided. Experiment with each and find what causes the readings to change.
2. Although each is connected to the Phidgets interface kit as an analogue sensor, is the full range of values really needed and/or used? Consider whether a reading detects a continuous value or is drawn from a small set of states.
3. Consider the response time of the sensors. Adjust your program from lab 1.6 to record a series of readings over time; running each experiment several times. Consider how various sensors respond:

   light: switch LEDs to get controlled timing; use different numbers of and coloured LEDs to see how the readings vary, isolating from ambient light if possible;
   force, magnetic, vibration, IR reflective, touch: see if quick / gentle / distant stimuli are missed;
   light, force, magnetic, temperature, touch: does it take time to build to a stable reading?
   light, force, magnetic, vibration, temperature, touch: does it take time to revert to an ambient reading after a controlled stimulus?

4. Record your timings and readings in a spreadsheet. Draw graphs, with error bars, consider repeatability especially where human stimulus is required.
5. Collect a series of timed samples and note the conditions. Save these sensor logs in file(s), for future use.
6. You might want to try and identify the sensor components in use (the Phidgets web site has some data, which can then be used to find manufacturers' data sheets) and see how your findings correspond to the expected parameters of the components.

5.9 Laboratory Exercises: Process Sensor Data and Describe Context

The purpose of this lab is to consider how to describe meaning associated with sensor input.

1. Consider the sensors you have. What do they measure? What is the physical space which they sense?
2. Building on lab 5.8 consider the range of raw readings the sensor provides. What conditions do they correspond to?
3. Identify any gaps or shortcomings in the raw representation.
4. Construct an ontology to describe the property, either building on or as an alternative to 5.2. Are the definitions unambiguous, are there any synonyms or grey areas?
5. Construct a mapping between the raw data and the ontology. Are there any gaps or overlaps in the mappings?

6. Program this mapping, so that you can display both the raw data and the high level description. How complex is this program? How flexible are the definitions?
7. For further work you might want to consider feedback systems which allow users to develop, extend or correct the mapping from readings to ontologies. Would having multiple readings help to define any conditions?

References

1. Abowd, G.D., Mynatt, E.D.: Charting past, present, and future research in ubiquitous computing. ACM Trans. Comput.-Hum. Interact. **7**(1), 29–58 (2000)
2. Abowd, G.D., Atkeson, C.G., Hong, J.I., Long, S., Kooper, R., Pinkerton, M.: Cyberguide: a mobile context-aware tour guide. Wirel. Netw. **3**(5), 421–433 (1997)
3. Beigl, M., Krohn, A., Zimmer, T., Decker, C.: Typical sensors needed in ubiquitous and pervasive computing. In: First International Workshop on Networked Sensing Systems (INSS '04), SICE, Tokyo (2004)
4. Brown, P.J., Bovey, J.D., Chen, X.: Context-aware applications: from the laboratory to the marketplace. IEEE Pers. Commun. **4**(5), 58–64 (1997)
5. Chalmers, D.: Contextual Mediation to Support Ubiquitous Computing. PhD thesis, Imperial College, London, UK (2002)
6. Chalmers, D., Dulay, N., Sloman, M.: A framework for contextual mediation in mobile and ubiquitous computing. Pers. Ubiquitous Comput. **8**(1), 1–18 (2004)
7. Chen, H., Finin, T., Joshi, A.: An ontology for context-aware pervasive computing environments. Knowl. Eng. Rev. **18**, 197–207 (2003). Special Issue on Ontologies for Distributed Systems
8. Dey, A.K., Abowd, G.D.: Towards a better understanding of context and context-awareness. In: Workshop on the What, Who, Where, When, and How of Context-Awareness, Conference on Human Factors in Computer Systems (CHI2000) (2000)
9. Dey, A.K., Abowd, G.D., Salber, D.: A conceptual framework and a toolkit for supporting the rapid prototyping of context-aware applications. Hum.-Comput. Interact. **16**(2, 3, 4), 97–166 (2001)
10. Dourish, P.: What we talk about when we talk about context. Pers. Ubiquitous Comput. **8**(1), 19–30 (2004)
11. Gellersen, H.W., Schmidt, A., Beigl, M.: Multi-sensor context-awareness in mobile devices and smart artifacts. Mob. Netw. Appl. **7**(5), 341–351 (2002)
12. Harle, R.K., Hopper, A.: Deploying and evaluating a location-aware system. In: Shin, K.G., Kotz, D., Noble, B.D. (eds.) MobiSys, pp. 219–232. ACM, New York (2005)
13. Harter, A., Hopper, A., Steggles, P., Ward, A., Webster, P.: The anatomy of a context-aware application. Wirel. Netw. **8**(2–3), 187–197 (2002)
14. Henricksen, K., Indulska, J., Rankotonirainy, A.: Modeling context information in pervasive computing systems. In: Pervasive, Zurich, Switzerland, pp. 167–180 (2002)
15. Henricksen, K., Indulska, J.: A software engineering framework for context-aware pervasive computing. In: PerCom, pp. 77–86. IEEE Computer Society, Washington (2004)
16. O'Neill, E., Kostakos, V., Kindberg, T., Fatah den. Schieck, A., Penn, A., Fraser, D.S., Jones, T.: Instrumenting the city: developing methods for observing and understanding the digital cityscape. In: Dourish, P., Friday, A. (eds.) Ubicomp. Lecture Notes in Computer Science, vol. 4206, pp. 315–332. Springer, Berlin (2006)
17. Petrelli, D., Not, E., Strapparava, C., Stock, O., Zancanaro, M.: Modeling context is like taking pictures. In: Workshop on the What, Who, Where, When, Why and How of Context-Awareness at CHI2000, The Hague, Holland (2000)
18. Ranganathan, A., Al-Muhtadi, J., Campbell, R.H.: Reasoning about uncertain contexts in pervasive computing environments. IEEE Pervasive Comput. **3**(2), 62–70 (2004)

19. Ranganathan, A., Campbell, R.H.: An infrastructure for context-awareness based on first order logic. Pers. Ubiquitous Comput. **7**(6), 353–364 (2003)
20. Salber, D., Dey, A.K., Abowd, G.D.: The context toolkit: aiding the development of context-enabled applications. In: CHI, pp. 434–441 (1999)
21. Schilit, B.N., Adams, N., Want, R.: Context-aware computing applications. In: IEEE Workshop on Mobile Computing Systems and Applications (1994)
22. Schmidt, A.: Ubiquitous Computing—Computing in Context. PhD thesis, Lancaster University, UK (2002)
23. Schmidt, A., Aidoo, K.A., Takaluoma, A., Tuomela, U., van Laerhoven, K., van de Velde, W.: Advanced interaction in context. In: 1st Intl. Symposium on Handheld and Ubiquitous Computing (HUC), Karlsruhe, Germany (1999)
24. Sloman, M., Lupu, E.: Policy specification for programmable networks. In: Covaci, S. (ed.) IWAN. Lecture Notes in Computer Science, vol. 1653, pp. 73–84. Springer, Berlin (1999)
25. Smith, M.K., Welty, C., McGuinness, D.L.: Owl web ontology language guide. Technical report, W3C (2004)
26. Strang, T., Linnhoff-Popien, C.: A context modeling survey. In: Workshop on Advanced Context Modelling, Reasoning and Management at UbiComp (2004)
27. Tulloch, S. (ed.): The Oxford English Dictionary. Oxford University Press, Oxford (1995)
28. Wood, K.R., Richardson, T., Bennett, F., Harter, A., Hopper, A.: Global teleporting with Java: toward ubiquitous personalized computing. IEEE Comput. **30**(2), 53–59 (1997)

Chapter 6
Error in Sensed Data

In Chap. 5 we introduced sensing the world in order to behave in a more appropriate way to the context of use. Of course, interfacing to the real world is imprecise, the domain of engineering trade-offs and things (e.g. people) outside of systems designers' control.

In this chapter we shall examine why sensors may provide incorrect data; how these problems may be corrected, allowed for, or presented.

6.1 Sources of Error and Uncertainty

First, we shall examine why not all sensor readings tell us precisely what we want to know. There are several possible reasons for this, which we shall examine in turn.

6.1.1 Device Error

Firstly, there is the simple case of a failure of the device. This may be a failure of the sensor component, its interface circuits, its connection to the processor, or the driver software. It is not, generally, easy to tell which situation has occurred. For most devices and circuits common failure modes are well understood; but having put these systems into the real world we must also consider failure due to external forces, e.g. moisture and vibration. Often individual components will fail as an open circuit or short circuit and remain failed. Occasionally failure will result in random behaviour or oscillations.

Failure need not be absolute. There may also be temporary or intermittent problems with a device. Problems due to manufacturing processes, e.g. dry solder joints, may be exacerbated by vibration or temperature changes. Similar effects can be created by moisture causing a short circuit, which then disappears when the device drys out. These cases will often appear as intermittent function.

D. Chalmers, *Sensing and Systems in Pervasive Computing*,
Undergraduate Topics in Computer Science,
DOI 10.1007/978-0-85729-841-6_6, © Springer-Verlag London Limited 2011

A lack of power can also result in a lack of function, particularly when the sensor is powered separately to the processor, which is then fixed by charging. However, power sources running low can also result in changes to the response for a given stimulus; scaling and offset of readings; and changes to oscillator dependent behaviours. These are much harder to differentiate from correct readings than simple failures which give boundary readings.

Another problem which can result in both incorrect assumptions about device response and temporary "failure" is sensor stimulus approaching or beyond device or circuit design limits. Many circuits have a non-linear region as readings approach the limit of response. Once inputs have gone beyond design limits a saturated response in usually achieved, although typically the actual property can carry on varying, e.g. a light sensor designed for day-time natural light levels being used under bright lights or at night.

6.1.2 Deployment Issues

Deployment issues can either be quite radical or quite subtle, and also intermittent. Essentially the problem is a disconnect between the sensor and the (intended / required) property of the object.

All sensors require that a property is transferred from the object in question to the sensor device. The quality of the transfer is critical: is there any distortion or loss in the measurement? Is the object of interest the only one which is being measured, or are measurements combined, e.g. by detecting motion for all in a room and assuming that all people are moving similarly? The positioning and attachment of sensor devices, and their sensitivity across space must be understood to properly interpret the sensor data. Gaps in sensor response form part of the game in [2]. This can be supported by well designed middleware which allows selection of appropriate sensors and good meta-data. However, in an environment where sensors are mobile, or simply not precisely deployed and maintained, this knowledge is hard to obtain. Even problems as simple and inevitable as oxidation, dirt falling on optical sensors and sticky tape becoming loose can create a disconnect between sensor and intended object of sensing.

Further, measured properties may be a secondary effect or the measurement of some proxy. For instance, many sensors' response varies with temperature (secondary effect); or location may be measured by some tag (proxy) intended to be associated with a person [18], but sometimes left behind.

Next we shall consider a range of problems which can affect sensors, even when they are operating normally and correctly focused on the object of interest.

6.1.3 Noise

By "noise" we refer to small fluctuations in the signal. This noise typically arises from some combination of: real (but unnoticed) variation reported by over-sensitive sensors; electrical interference, particularly from mains electricity either inducing current in cables or devices, or from poorly earthed or smoothed power supplies; and minor instability in sensor design. Good electronic design and installation to avoid sources of interference are key here. Some noise is random and so hard to remove once introduced; while some is predictable and may be filtered at the cost of additional circuitry or software processing (discussed in Sect. 6.2).

6.1.4 Processing Errors

Analogue to digital converters can introduce errors. Driver code can further distort readings if they convert non-linear data to a normalised scale. The latter problems may come from sources including changes of scale (bit width, units) between input and output and associated rounding and interpolation errors; and transformation of readings using approximate functions. Generally these errors will be small and predictable. Errors due to ADC accuracy etc. may be treated as for electrical noise.

6.1.5 Variations Between Sensors

Multiple sensors of the same type may be used either to allow redundancy (see also below) or to sense different objects for comparison. Clearly there are a range of parts which might be used to sense any given property, quite properly giving rise to different behaviours. The difference between parts of different specification can be resolved by knowing what parts are present. Unfortunately multiple instances of the same part vary, even within the same production run—typical tolerances range from 0.1% to 5%, with many examples beyond this in either direction. As a typical sensor, even a simple voltage divider like many of the Phidgets sensors, relies on multiple components to create and process the signal this variation can be more complex than is immediately apparent. This effect is magnified by differences in attachment to the object being sensed. Together these differences make absolute comparisons between two objects, or binding to similar sensors fixed in the environment by a mobile user hard and fragile. Careful calibration can resolve this problem, but it is hard to maintain careful calibration of millions of long-lived sensors which are embedded in lived spaces and/or are mobile.

6.1.6 Old Data

Some context sensing uses predictive sources, such as diaries, to describe what is expected. Obviously predictions may be inaccurate, people suffer delays and interruptions, and so older information is more subject to change than new information, which explains in part our keenness to automatically sense context rather than have the user provide it. Old data can also be a problem where sensor readings are only occasional to save on collection and distribution costs.

Sensor data can also be made obsolete by changes in the user's context, particularly location. If a user moves away from a sensor having taken a reading its value will only continue to be accurate as far as the environment described by the sensor extends: room level sensor scope is one of the most noticeable seams in the sensor's model of the world. A further, very common, example is moving out of range of GPS signals, which are easily blocked by buildings and dense vegetation. In both cases it would be wise to have sensor data expire, either when location has changed or after some time without gaining a new reading, or if a reading has been static longer than is deemed plausible.

6.1.7 Obfuscation

We tend to concentrate here on understanding, quantifying, removing and adjusting for error. However, a reverse process is also possible: *obfuscation*. This is the process of deliberately hiding the real situation, often to preserve privacy. Changes in reporting granularity (e.g. time, precision) and mimicking natural errors (e.g. delay, noise, offset) are usual techniques. This requires that the introduced error cannot simply be filtered out and that the resulting reports are believable; in some cases there is a desire to mask the obfuscation, in others it may be plain that the data is not as detailed as it might be. We will not discuss the creation of these effects further here, but ought to be alive to the possibility that some errors in received data are deliberately introduced. Wishart et al. [19] discusses these issues further.

6.1.8 Influence of Sensors on Environment

The final source of "error" we should consider is not error so much as unplanned change. It is quite possible that the sensor may influence the property that it is trying to measure. For instance, current passing through a thermistor causes the thermistor to become warm, thus affecting the measurement. LEDs on devices emit light, which light detectors then detect. On a more complex level, the awareness of sensors may alter people's behaviour. The strongest systems impact of this is that when devices are first installed people's behaviour around them may well be different to that once they have faded from conscious thought, resulting in skew of any training data or installation calibration; similarly people may develop habits that cause systems to behave as they want which are not entirely natural (and not necessarily based on a proper model of the system).

6.1.9 Summary

In processing and using context data we have a series of problems to addressed, many of which also arise in sensor networks.

1. Device error and failure
2. Device saturation
3. Processing error
4. Deployment error: transparency of sensor's connection to object
5. Deployment error: strength of association between object and sensor
6. Electrical and other random noise
7. Variation between parts
8. Obsolescence
9. Obfuscation
10. Sensors' effect on people and environment

In the following sections we shall examine ways to address some of these problems.

6.2   Handling Noise in Sensors

It is clearly desirable to minimise the impact of error on our systems, either by correcting the data or ignoring data which is erroneous. However, not all of the sources of error we have identified can be handled by any single mechanism; and it is not always possible to detect errors or differentiate one sort of error from another. At the same time, it is desirable to have systems react in a timely fashion to real changes in the sensed world—for real pervasive computing systems we need to work with current and past sensor values.

Many of the techniques we shall apply below make assumptions about the behaviour of errors. Identifying saturation values or describing them as more likely to contain inaccuracy requires an understanding of where a sensor saturates; removing noise requires a model of how the error is distributed (often assuming a *normal* distribution); adjusting for variation and deployment variations requires a reference point which is believed. When applying any error *filtering* mechanism (especially those for removing noise) some information and/or timeliness will be lost. It is important to understand the characteristics of the data, the noise, the filter mechanism and the application's use of the information in order to be confident that the loss of information is not excessive.

In Fig. 6.1 we present a series of example sensor readings. Each trace illustrates a pattern of change, showing the underlying real value and a trace of sample values from single synthetic sensor. The signal patterns illustrated are: step change, gradual change, step change to a saturated value (0), and events which are described by a pair of sensor readings each. Each of these traces includes Gaussian error at a moderate level to make the effect clear for illustration, and also a small number of outliers with a higher level of Gaussian noise. The distribution of error from the

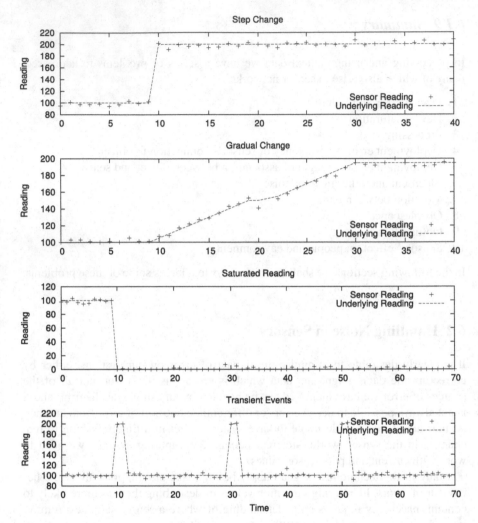

Fig. 6.1 A set of example sensor readings

signal for the step change model sensors is illustrated in Fig. 6.2—which shows a classic Gaussian distribution as far as the volume of data allows.

The traces illustrate common forms of signal in one dimension—plainly multiple dimensions can exhibit similar behaviours, e.g. in location, acceleration, but are slightly harder to illustrate on the page. One complication with multiple dimension data that should be remembered is that signals may arrive in several dimensions at once and that the error may not be independent across the channels, however the techniques described remain useful and any dependence in dimensions can be factored in.

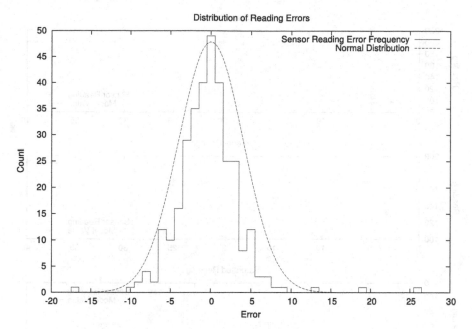

Fig. 6.2 Distribution of error in example sensor readings

6.2.1 Averaging

Possibly the most obvious approach to noise and small variations between multiple sensors is to take an average. The recent past is a useful indicator of the current state of the world and we can usually sense faster than real changes occur. Even here there are a number of options, each of which introduces its own artefacts into the signal. The simplest case is of a single sensor. Here we show two options: averaging over a number of readings and taking an exponentially weighted moving average (EWMA).

In a simple average we have to pick the number of samples to consider. This can be derived from the expected noise patterns, e.g. to reduce the effect of infrequent large errors in a slowly changing signal a larger number of samples must be averaged than where handling frequent small errors; alternatively the history size might be chosen to reduce the effect of old data, balancing size with sample frequency; or the limit might be set by available memory for holding the history. Having chosen a history length a mean can be taken; although alternatives are possible, as discussed below.

$$hmean_t = \sum_{x=t-n+1}^{t} reading_x / n \qquad (6.1)$$

The n values must all be initialised, either by re-using the first sample or by collecting n samples, before the result will be usable.

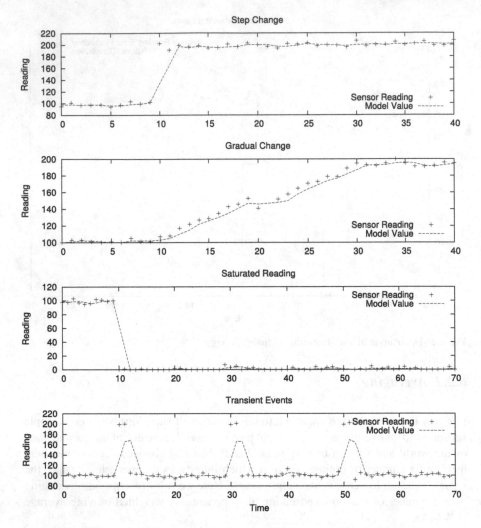

Fig. 6.3 A model generated from example sensor readings: average of 3 value history

The effect of a 3 value history model on our example data patterns is illustrated in Fig. 6.3. It can be seen that the model value tracks a slowly changing sensor trace quite closely, but that there is a delay in responding to step changes and that transients are "squashed"—reduced in magnitude but stretched over time. Once a steady state has been reached in the real values (without noise) there is some variation as the short history is perturbed by noise, but rather smaller than the noise. A longer history would provide a stronger filter for noise but exacerbate the delayed reaction effects.

The cost of this model is:

- To store the model: n (3 in the example) sample values and a pointer to the next store value to replace
- To add a reading: update the stored value and next value pointer
- To compute a new model value: access and sum the n stored values and divide

An alternative processing model is the Exponentially Weighted Moving Average (EWMA). This is commonly used where computing resources are limited and maintaining a large volume of state or performing large average calculations is undesirable. In this case the previous average ($ewma_{t-1}$) value and a new reading ($reading_t$) are combined in a set ratio (α):

$$ewma_t = \alpha.ewma_{t-1} + (1 - \alpha).reading_t \tag{6.2}$$

The tuning decision to be made here is on the ratio, where too slow an update causes old readings to have an impact when they have become obsolete, while too fast an update causes unwanted noise to be shown in the model. Values for α are typically between 0.01 and 0.3, depending on noise filtering and update speed required. A value of $1/8$ is used in some situations to allow a shift to be used to perform the division with integer arithmetic. The model must be initialised with a value before a usable result is obtained; using several samples improves the quality of this model.

The effect on our example data patterns is illustrated in Fig. 6.4 (we discuss deviation in Sect. 6.2.3). We can see here that the initial values are not perturbed by noise much, but that the choice of α here results in rather a slow update. The curve as the model converges on the underlying reading is characteristic of the EWMA process, much as a linear approach to the underlying reading is characteristic of the explicit history and mean model. The slow convergence is exacerbated where a value saturates, as there may well be no noise beyond the saturation value (e.g. 0) to "pull" the model towards reality. The transient events model shows a quick but small response to the event, but a long time is taken to return to the lower value.

The cost of this model is:

- To store the model: a single value
- To add a reading: two divisions and an addition
- To compute a new model value: no action, the value is computed by adding

6.2.2 Using Multiple Sensors

In both the above cases managing the model is more complex when there are multiple sensors. If multiple sensors are sampled round-robin and applied in sequence then the later sensors will have a stronger effect on an EWMA than the earlier sensors. If the history size is not a multiple of the number of sensors then simple averages will not reflect a natural combination of readings. If some sensors report more frequently than others then they will have a greater effect than other sensors in both models. Both these last two problems can be addressed for simple averages by having a vector of sensor readings addressed by sensor ID rather than a simple history;

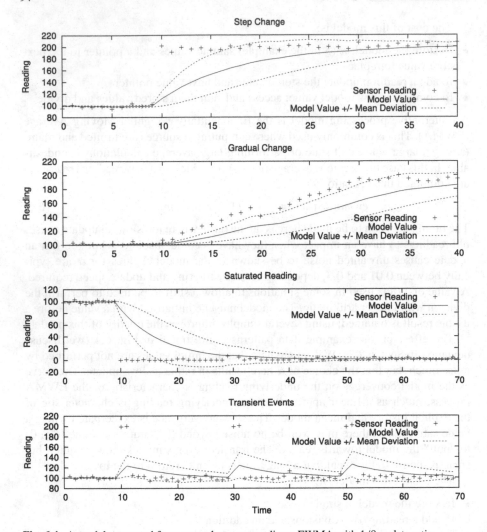

Fig. 6.4 A model generated from example sensor readings: EWMA with 1/8 update ratio

however this does not apply to EWMAs and requires that the current set of valid sensors is known and maintained.

Another averaging technique addresses the problem of slow reaction to change and also that of sensor reliability: take samples from multiple sensors. Where noise arises randomly within sensing systems multiple sources will tend to cancel out. Where noise arises in the environment then little gain can be expected. We illustrate this as a simple average from the last values at each sensor, but the approach can be combined with other approaches for greater filtering of noise and with voting

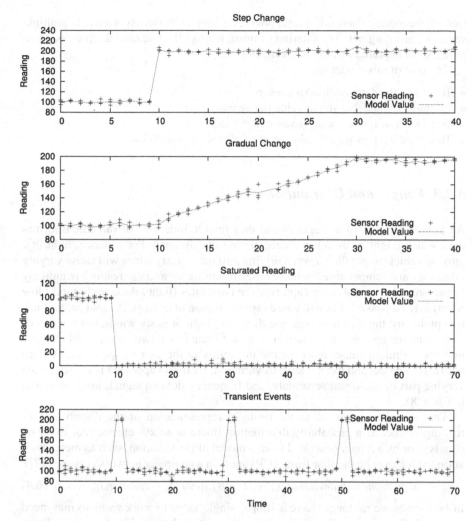

Fig. 6.5 A model generated from example sensor readings: average of 3 independent sensors

algorithms and time-stamped values to better handle sensor failure and different positioning of sensors.

$$mean = \sum_{x=1}^{n} sensor(x)/n \qquad (6.3)$$

A reading is needed from each sensor to initialise.

The effect on our example data patterns is illustrated in Fig. 6.5. To generate this graph we created two additional sensor streams with the same underlying values as the rest of the examples but fresh random noise. One of these streams also suffers from a small offset. It can be seen from the various traces that the reported model follows the underlying value well but that there are still small but obvious fluctuations in the model. There are several obvious examples of Gaussian noise in multiple sensors cancelling out. The filtering of noise is less effective than the previous two models, but capture of transients is much better.

The cost of this model is:

- To collect the data: additional sensors
- To store the model: a single value per sensor
- To add a reading: replacing a value in the store
- To compute a new model value: sum of all values and divide

6.2.3 Ranges and Distribution

An alternative view of averages is that they tend to hide a lot of valuable information, which might be useful in characterising the situation. For instance, light in a moving vehicle might flicker when driving past trees; gusty winds will cause varying vibrations and temperature. In these cases reporting an average reading is unlikely to capture either actual state; capturing the two states (light / dark, high wind / low wind) may be possible but will cause rapid variation of context. A rapid capture has two problems: the user may perceive flickering light or gusty winds, not a series of states; and the response to context may be different in the two cases, rapid changes in response might cause unacceptable instability in the user's experience. A third option is to model and use the level of variation. (A fourth approach is to look at the varying part of the signal separately, and frequency domain signals are considered in Chap. 8).

This model of variation might be by a representation of the distribution of readings, either as a probability distribution (there is an x% chance that the state equals y) or by a range, generated from a model of the variation, such as mean deviation (which may be familiar from TCP timers in a computer networks course [17]).

$$deviation_t = \beta.deviation_{t-1} + (1 - \beta).|(ewma_t - reading_t)| \qquad (6.4)$$

In both cases we no longer have a simple single value to work with, so may need to take different approaches to handling the context data. In Fig. 6.4 you will see a mean deviation plotted around the model values, indicating one model of "noisiness". It is easy to see periods of "change", where the EWMA is further from the observed values the deviation becomes wider. The change is in the model, which as we have seen may take some time to converge on the readings. The range described by the deviation around the mean includes the real readings much faster than the mean, which for step change, saturation and transient events spends some time indicating a value which is not and has not (recently) been the actual value recorded but some intermediate value. Rather than use the mean directly we could use the range described around the mean as the value; or the variation may be treated as a separate parameter. In interpreting range data probabilistic or fuzzy logic models may be appropriate; in general a higher level translation or use of the sensor data must consider whether the error level model causes a change in behaviour or in the specificity of the higher level value (e.g. from an ontology) reported.

6.2.4 Averaging with Change Detection

The tension between responsiveness and noise immunity in the average models is clear. One approach to handling this is to maintain two readings: a stable one and a fast response one [5, 12]. The difference between the two readings can be used as a change detector: if there is a significant difference then the variation is not caused by noise but by real change. The stable reading can be used in most situations. The responsive reading can be used, when change is detected, as a latest value to re-seed the stable model. The downside of this system is that three parameters are needed: update ratios / history lengths for the stable and responsive readings and a trigger ratio for change detection. The latter is most sensitive to knowledge of likely changes and noise distribution, in order to avoid false detection or failure to detect change.

Other methods that might be applied are the variation of the update ratio, possibly according to a measure of variation; change in sampling frequency in response to a measure of sampling variation (to speed conversion on a changed value); and filtering of outliers (although a large change needs to be differentiated from a series of outliers).

The effect on our example data patterns is illustrated in Fig. 6.6. In this model we use the 3 value history and $1/8$ EWMA update ratios as before. The jump threshold in this case is one mean deviation. An alternative threshold might be a percentage of the model value, but this would require tuning to the expected noise level. So the model reports:

$$\textbf{if } |ewma_t - hmean_t| < deviation_{t-1} \textbf{ then } ewma_t = hmean_t \qquad (6.5)$$

Having corrected the ewma, this can be reported as the model value and the deviation updated. It can be seen that in most cases the traces resemble the EWMA traces but that under step changes the linear 3-value history curve is adopted. The low level noise filtering in particular is as good as the EWMA while the tracking of gradual changes is as good as the history model. The transient signal still suffers, as it did in both of the underlying models. The deviation model is also shown and it can be seen that this usefully indicates a recent significant change or represents the noise level. Here a more responsive update ratio (than the EWMA) might better indicate ongoing changes in the model.

- The sum of the two models (here, history and EWMA), plus
- To add a reading: calculation of the models as normal, then an additional comparison and possibly an additional store to reset the less sensitive one.

6.2.5 Kalman Filters

The Kalman filter is discussed in many more mathematical books and courses and is one of the class of *Bayesian* filters. We refer the mathematical reader back to

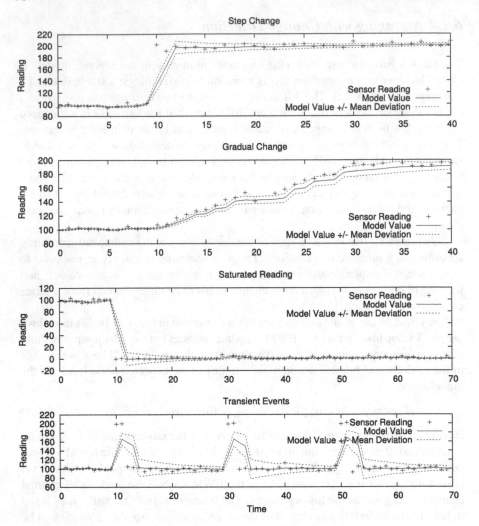

Fig. 6.6 A model generated from example sensor readings: EWMA with 4 value history quick response

Gelb's text [8] as this is suitably practical for the approach here and the more applied computing reader to [7] for a good overview of the maths and use of Bayesian filters in Pervasive computing. In brief: The Kalman filter describes a system with readings (z_i) of a possibly varying underlying state (x) each of which contains Gaussian noise ($z_i = x + v_i$), which is a development beyond the smoothing of a single state that methods such as a mean give. It does not require a certain number of readings or the pattern of readings from multiple sources to be controlled. A Kalman filter provides an estimate ($\hat{x}$) of the underlying state. This model is used to extrapolate the next expected step, which is then updated with a reading. It is optimised to give a minimised mean square error, where the mean error is zero and not related to the underlying value of x—where the error pattern is Gaussian this will hold. A normal distribution is common, but not always the case, for example many models of human activity and computer networks show a long-tailed distribution. A linear model of the expected variation is required, which is limiting where this is complex to describe in advance or where the variation is not linear. A well chosen model of variation allows a significant improvement over the averaging models, in particular in response to lag. It also allows us to extract derivative information from a series of noisy readings as well as modelling the reported values themselves, rather than deriving the additional information from the model of reported values. Multiple sensors may also be used as input, informing related aspects of the state model, which can be used to check each other and aid in predicting variation, e.g. speed allows checking of reasonable changes in location.

6.2.6 Particle Filters

The Particle filter solves a similar problem to the Kalman filter, although it does not have the limitation of linear change. Here the state of the system is modelled as a probability density function, with values represented by weighted particles. An early introduction bringing work in this area together is found in [3], although it is not the first work to use a probability density function represented by particles. The trade-off is in computational complexity. The approach is different: rather than a closed loop equation the particle filter represents the possible states with a set of "particles", each representing a possible value. The particles can be imagined to show a histogram of the likelihood that a particular state is the current state—imagine Fig. 6.2 represents the weighting of a set of particles. These are used to predict the next state. The prediction is corrected with a measurement of the state and the set of particles updated so that the density of particles around the measured state tends to increase. At each update step the histogram is revised, to better reflect increased knowledge and any changes in state. Some randomness can be introduced in the sampling, to avoid the model collapsing around a single value and being unable to respond properly to change. The accuracy of the model depends on the number of particles, and hence the state being retained. Applied use of particle filters is described further in [11, 15] and an interactive demonstration of the particle filter can be found at[1].

The process for building a particle filter is, in outline:

1. A set of *initial particles* are generated. In our example we distributed these equally across the valid range of readings and then discarded the first few results while the filter stabilised. We used 100 particles, although useful results can be had with fewer a greater number will give a better model.

---

[1]http://www.oursland.net/projects/particlefilter/.

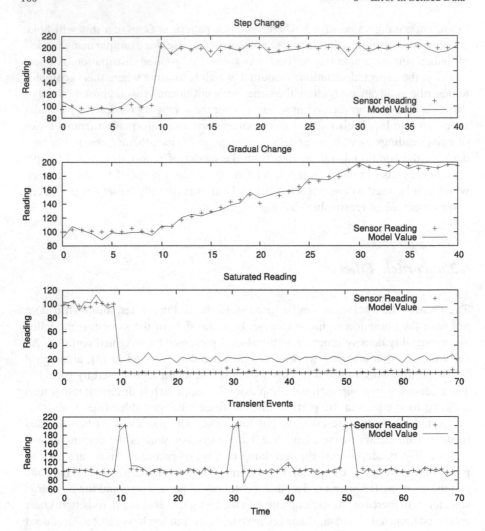

Fig. 6.7 A model generated from example sensor readings: particle filter

2. Each particle has a weight, the likelihood of it being correct in a given distribution around sample. The distribution of noise in our example is Gaussian which
   is reflected in the model, but other models of variation can be accommodated.
   In our initialisation (not shown) we gave all particles the same weight, faster
   convergence could be achieved using a Gaussian model around the first sample.
3. Then, on each step:
   a. Find the importance weight of each particle $w_t^{(j)} = p(z_t|x_{t-1}^{(j)})$, given the sam-
      ple z_t.
   b. Randomly sample n particles from x_{t-1}, with a distribution according their
      weight, i.e. $p(x_t|x_{t-1})$. Any knowledge of expected change in value can be
      applied in the distribution at this step, by adjusting the probability.

c. Inject a small amount of noise into particles to stop collapse around a single value or failure to generate particle values from the current set when the observed value goes outside an over-accurate model. This *degenerate* model problem is found particularly when the underlying system is prone to transients or step changes. This step is not present in all versions of the algorithm, in systems with sufficient noise and an appropriate model of change the previous resampling step is sufficient to avoid degeneracy.

d. Normalise weights of particles so that the total weight is 1.

e. Estimate the value to be reported, e.g. by taking the mean of the resulting distribution.

If higher level context values can be described as (Gaussian) distributions of probability on the value space then a comparison between particles and these distributions can be made and the most likely higher level value can be reported. This allows the particle filter to combine several important ideas into one algorithm:

- Modelling noise in the signal.
- Modelling derivative information and multi-sensor systems and using other parameters of the model to inform the expected next value of a given parameter, e.g. location informed by speed.
- Converting from raw numeric sensor data to higher level conceptual data, moving up the context stack.

As can be seen from Fig. 6.7 the model can follow the signal very well, for a wide range of signals. We included no assumptions about patterns of change in our model, but if rates of change, sizes of real changes etc were known this information could be incorporated. The variation due to the granularity of just 100 particles being used, the model observing the noise in the signal and due to noise injected in the model can be seen—further tuning can lead to a more stable model. However on a larger scale the model follows the sensor readings well. Where the value saturates to zero the model fails to completely saturate as zero is the lowest value expected. However, the real issues with this model are the need to make assumptions about the expected variations and the higher computational complexity of the model, including significant store requirements, floating point arithmetic and the need to generate random numbers.

The cost of this model is:

- To store the model: a floating point value for each particle.
- To add a reading: generating weights according to the sample, random sampling of particles, introduction of variation model and normalisation.
- To compute a new model value, computing this model over the set of particles.

6.2.7 Summary

Each of the filtering models shown uses a different approach to computing a model of reality from noisy samples. Each has their place in this text by occupying different places in the solution space. This space has several dimensions:

Table 6.1 RMS error for filters and example samples

| Data Set | RMS Error For Filter | | | | |
	History	EWMA	Avg 3 Sensors	EWMA and History	Particle
Step	11.9	29.1	2.4	11.8	7.1
Slope	4.4	19.0	1.6	6.8	4.3
Saturate	9.0	21.8	1.7	9.0	19.4
Events	22.0	25.5	2.4	22.5	6.9

- Memory and computational requirements
- Responsiveness to rapid changes in signal
- Strength of filtering applied to noise
- Quality of representation of uncertainty in the model

The choice of algorithm depends on the value of these properties in the system and the expected data's properties.

In Table 6.1 we compare the RMS error for each model in each of our synthetic scenarios. When reading this comparison it must be remembered that this is a sample comparison, in particular:

- The models have not had any significant tuning and have the same configuration for each data set. In a real deployment greater care to match configuration with signal characteristics should be taken.
- RMS error does not tell the whole story, occasional large mistakes are expensive but cannot be told apart from many small errors. Improving on this is left for the interested reader in lab Exercise 6.8.
- The values presented are for the example illustrated. Different runs with different data will give somewhat different results.

Despite these shortcomings it is clear that deploying multiple sensors or supporting the complexity of more sophisticated techniques such as a particle filter is worthwhile in many situations. The particle filter in this case fails to converge on zero on the saturated model affecting its result. Finer grained particles would help here. Of the simpler algorithms, EWMA performs poorly with the tuning chosen while the combined model improves this significantly, by using the short history value to reset the model where the difference between model and sample is greater than the mean deviation.

The proper choice of algorithm depends on the properties of the data and capacity in the deployment for tuning the algorithm and absorbing its computational, memory and sensor-use demands. For instance, despite the error levels seen here for some data sources and tunings these simpler algorithms represent an acceptable choice, particularly when processor cycles or memory are very limited. Despite any apparent quality shown here the examples serve more to illustrate the challenges different sorts of data present and the approaches commonly taken to filtering noise to build a model of low level values. The approaches presented here, combined with reading about additional filtering models in the literature and understanding how these models are translated up the context stack, should give you a starting point for better handling your own sensor data.

6.3 Fusion: Combining Sensors' Data

We noted above that combining readings from multiple sensors with single-sensor models presents problems with bias towards some sensors, currency of particular sensors and the possibility that some sensors might be exhibiting substantial errors while most are working normally.

6.3.1 Averaging

Averaging was considered earlier as a technique for filtering noise, but because of the cost of deploying additional sensors and the remaining noise in the model it is more properly considered as a data fusion technique. Averaging many readings with only slight variation (or few large variations), or which are distinctly out of phase in reporting, is reasonable. If sensors report at different rates care must be taken that the fused reading gives proper weight to the various sensors. Averaging where there is a significant disagreement between sensors risks describing the situation as a case which none of the sensors are experiencing. Consider a sensor which reads 10 and another which reads 90: the mean is 50, but if the scale is degrees Celsius then this response significantly mis-represents most human interpretations of either sensor reading. More complex statistical methods with more inputs may be less prone to this sort of error, but can still create trouble if the inputs are not consistent with the model's design, or the question asked of the model is poorly understood, or in pathological conditions (when inaccurate behaviour may well have the worst consequences).

6.3.2 Voting

Voting is an alternative model, with a long history in reliable systems design for safety critical systems involving sensors. In essence the principle is to over-provision (which is often possible with the pervasive computing vision) and to take a view based on a defined majority (the degree of majority can be defined for greater reliability and failure to decide can be signalled to the user). The *Byzantine Generals Problem* [14] allows for sensors which have failed while still giving plausible readings, so is applicable to many of our error cases.

Voting algorithms are usually framed as deciding amongst a set of well-defined discrete values. This is therefore appropriate for higher level context models. For low level values on a fine-grained continuous scale subject to noise absolute agreement is harder, here the vote may be on exclusion of outliers in order to form a better average, range, or distribution model.

6.3.3 Summary

As we have discussed, two sensors which are working normally might give different readings, due to deployment; manufacturing variation or design. These differences can manifest themselves as a constant offset; variation in saturation levels; a variation in stimulus—response relationship; a variation in timeliness; or a variation in the noise experienced. If the design and deployment are well understood then these can be compensated for. If there are many sensors then averaging or voting become appropriate. If some sensors are better trusted than others then other sensors can be interpreted relative to these. Otherwise it may well be best to *ask the user*—not about every reading, but to confirm what their interpretation of the situation is, to provide the necessary information to normalise the various readings.

6.4 Specifying Behaviour Despite Uncertainty

Sensed and processed context data are only ever a model for what we believe the users' situation is. However many sensors are used and however many readings are taken there is a possibility that the data will be inaccurate or miss some feature. However carefully we model the situation the translation from sensed data to context information is a fallible model, the model itself may not completely or correctly express the current user experience. It is therefore necessary to define a scope for the design of context aware systems and include mechanisms for handling error and uncertainty in the context model or the response to context.

Even in 1992 the active badge project [18] was addressing the problem of incorrect and old readings. Where users were moving a percentage probability that the location was correct was shown; where a user had not been sighted by the system for over 5 minutes, e.g. had gone out or switched the badge off, then the last location and a time or day were shown. This is a pragmatic programmed response to ageing data.

Some of the approaches to managing sensor data presented allow us to treat sensed data as a point value and others do not. In some cases a point value is useful, but a range or probability distribution is harder to use, e.g. "when the oven reaches 180° send a message to put the cake mixture in". In many other cases the behaviour is defined by a range-based semantics, e.g. "when within office-building use office-network". This latter form can easily accommodate uncertain data, and relations can also be defined over this style of data.

Adding sophistication to the "matching to cause behaviour" approach, we might wish to place a required confidence, or probability of correctness, on the data to cause a behaviour. This then allows us to construct hierarchies of behaviour specification, with safe, more general behaviours defined—in particular including "ask for help and sense again"—for less confident sensing situations and/or context sensed in an imprecise way, possibly holding many values. N.B. the two cases just mentioned are not necessarily the same: it is quite possible to be precise but lack confidence, or to confidently say the value lies somewhere in the possible range!

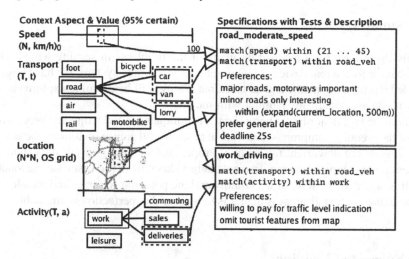

Fig. 6.8 Example of uncertainty in context used in specifications based on [4]. D. Chalmers, N. Dulay, and M. Sloman. Towards reasoning about context in the presence of uncertainty. In *Proceedings of Workshop on Advanced Context Modelling, Reasoning And Management at Ubi-Comp 2004*, 2004, http://itee.uq.edu.au/~pace/ContextWorkshop2004Program.html. Reprinted by permission

We may use models of confidence to describe a set of most likely values, using more general values is reflect a lack of confidence. Consider for instance the context models and specifications in Fig. 6.8, which reflect the contextual mediation of maps example in Table 5.1. Here we show an example of four context aspects, each of which has a value with some uncertainty (illustrated by a dashed box):

- speed of between 29 and 34 mph, possibly derived from recent motion changes
- most likely mode of transport is car or van, possibly derived from patterns of movement
- location within the dashed bounding box, possibly from GPS or cell-phone data
- an activity of making deliveries, possibly provided by the user

The combination of this context data causes two specifications to be activated, one for driving on road at moderate speed and one for driving for work. The are activated by tests for the context aspects (illustrated by a thin box around the value):

- speed of between 21 and 45 mph
- most likely mode of transport is on road
- location is used within the behaviour, not to identify a specification
- an activity of being at work

Different specifications may be activated at higher speeds, or if a van can be confidently identified as the mode of transport etc.

If the context model presents probability distributions, rather than these simple ranges, then matching between sensed distribution and models of situations may occur, as illustrated in [15].

6.5 Summary

In this chapter we have touched on many of the problems in sensing which arise from having to use real devices to interpret a very complex system. We have largely avoided reproducing mathematical texts, but it may well be useful to explore such a book if you are not already familiar with statistics.

There are two major issues here: Firstly, techniques for collecting and processing sensor data require compromises and are at best a useful approximation of the world, and at worst are downright misleading. Proper understanding of our data sources, processing and application requirements help to keep us in the first case. Secondly, that it is better to be aware of uncertainty and the potential for error and handle this in designing context awareness than it is to believe that perfection is attainable.

6.6 Suggested Readings

The following readings explore sensor error in context awareness further:

- Philip D. Gray and Daniel Salber. Modelling and using sensed context information in the design of interactive applications. In Murray Reed Little and Laurence Nigay, editors, *EHCI*, volume 2254 of *Lecture Notes in Computer Science*, pages 317–336. Springer, 2001
- S. Benford, R. Anastasi, M. Flintham, C. Greenhalgh, N. Tandavanitj, M. Adams, and J. Row-Farr. Coping with uncertainty in a location-based game. *Pervasive Computing, IEEE*, 2(3):34–41, July-Sept. 2003
- P. Korpipää, M. Koskinen, J. Peltola, S.-M. Mäkelä, and T. Seppänen. Bayesian approach to sensor-based context awareness. *Personal and Ubiquitous Computing*, 7(2):113–124, 2003
- K. Henricksen and J. Indulska. Modelling and using imperfect context information. In *Workshop on Context Modelling and Reasoning (CoMoRea'04)*, pages 33–37, Orlando, FL, USA, 2004
- A. Ranganathan, J. Al-Muhtadi, and R.H. Campbell. Reasoning about uncertain contexts in pervasive computing environments. *IEEE Pervasive Computing*, 3(2):62–70, 2004
- Amol Deshpande, Carlos Guestrin, and Samuel Madden. Using probabilistic models for data management in acquisitional environments. In *CIDR*, pages 317–328, 2005

The following concentrate on more complex noise filtering methods:

- Dieter Fox, Jeffrey Hightower, Lin Liao, Dirk Schulz, and Gaetano Borriello. Bayesian filtering for location estimation. *IEEE Pervasive Computing*, 2(3):24–33, 2003
- Donald Patterson, Lin Liao, Dieter Fox, and Henry Kautz. Inferring high-level behavior from low-level sensors. In *UbiComp 2003: Ubiquitous Computing*, pages 73–89. Springer, 2003

6.7 Laboratory Exercises: Tolerances and Calibration

This lab builds on lab 5.8. This exercise could usefully be started before the lab, as a seminar activity or home-work.

1. Identify a sensor which you have at least two of (light is a good candidate, but some variety is good). These could be two apparently identical parts or two different parts which measure the same property in the environment.
2. Get manufacturer's data sheet(s) for the sensor(s). Examine these to *predict* how sensors might vary. Consider both manufacturing tolerances and also how temperature and other effects cause variation (it is surprising how many electronic circuits double up as quite good thermometers). Consider how readings are taken: is there a simple value from an analogue to digital converter (ADC) or a time series? How might drivers and low-level processing introduce error?
3. Consider how this range of properties might require software correction to produce accurate readings with units. Consider how this range of properties could affect the mapping from low-level to high-level context, such as you produced in lab 5.9.
4. Devise an experiment to test the samples of this sensor that you have and find the actual variations. If you identified errors due to low-level processing, consider how you would test for these and the repeatability of any readings you take.
5. In the lab, run this experiment and write up your quantified results. Do two sensors routinely give the same response across a range of stimuli, e.g. brightness, orientation, colour? Consider the speed of response as well as absolute readings.
6. Compare filtering models such as averages and EWMAs, etc. Extend your program to run these statistics at run-time. What tuning does this need for these sensors? Can the ontology mapping from lab 5.9 be improved with this data? Consider the efficiency of your algorithms. What are the processing and memory requirements?

6.8 Laboratory Exercises: Building Filters

Consider the various noise filtering techniques described and explore the implications of test data and tuning filters.

1. Implement some small set of these
2. Generate some sample synthetic data streams
3. Test your filter algorithms against the synthetic streams. Is RMS error the most suitable measure? Would presenting more information averaged over several runs be informative? Try plotting cumulative error graphs for your models, as seen in [11], which tell you rather more about patterns of error.
4. Tune your filters to try and improve their results.
5. Test your filters with some real sensor data. Do they behave? Can you create synthetic models that provide a useful basis for testing filter algorithms?

References

1. Benford, S., Anastasi, R., Flintham, M., Greenhalgh, C., Tandavanitj, N., Adams, M., Row-Farr, J.: Coping with uncertainty in a location-based game. IEEE Pervasive Comput. **2**(3), 34–41 (2003)
2. Benford, S., Crabtree, A., Flintham, M., Drozd, A., Anastasi, R., Paxton, M., Tandavanitj, N., Adams, M., Row-Farr, J.: Can you see me now? ACM Trans. Comput.-Hum. Interact. **13**(1), 100–133 (2006)
3. Carpenter, J., Clifford, P., Fearnhead, P.: Improved particle filter for nonlinear problems. IEE Proc. Radar Sonar Navig. **146**(1), 2–7 (1999)
4. Chalmers, D., Dulay, N., Sloman, M.: Towards reasoning about context in the presence of uncertainty. In: Proceedings of Workshop on Advanced Context Modelling, Reasoning and Management at UbiComp 2004 (2004)
5. Chalmers, D., Sloman, M., Dulay, N.: Map adaptation for users of mobile systems. In: Proceedings of 10th Intl. World Wide Web Conference (WWW10), pp. 735–744. ACM, New York (2001)
6. Deshpande, A., Guestrin, C., Madden, S.: Using probabilistic models for data management in acquisitional environments. In: CIDR, pp. 317–328 (2005)
7. Fox, D., Hightower, J., Liao, L., Schulz, D., Borriello, G.: Bayesian filtering for location estimation. IEEE Pervasive Comput. **2**(3), 24–33 (2003)
8. Gelb, A.: Applied Optimal Estimation. MIT Press, Cambridge (1974)
9. Gray, P.D., Salber, D.: Modelling and using sensed context information in the design of interactive applications. In: Little, M.R., Nigay, L. (eds.) EHCI. Lecture Notes in Computer Science, vol. 2254, pp. 317–336. Springer, Berlin (2001)
10. Henricksen, K., Indulska, J.: Modelling and using imperfect context information. In: Workshop on Context Modelling and Reasoning (CoMoRea'04), Orlando, FL, USA, pp. 33–37 (2004)
11. Hightower, J., Borriello, G.: Particle filters for location estimation in ubiquitous computing: a case study. In: UbiComp 2004: Ubiquitous Computing, pp. 88–106. Springer, Berlin (2004)
12. Kim, M., Noble, B.D.: Mobile network estimation. In: 7th ACM Conference on Mobile Computing and Networking (MobiCom), Rome, Italy (2001)
13. Korpipää, P., Koskinen, M., Peltola, J., Mäkelä, S.-M., Seppänen, T.: Bayesian approach to sensor-based context awareness. Pers. Ubiquitous Comput. **7**(2), 113–124 (2003)
14. Lamport, L., Shostak, R., Pease, M.: The byzantine generals problem. ACM Trans. Program. Lang. Syst. **4**(3), 382–401 (1982)
15. Patterson, D., Liao, L., Fox, D., Kautz, H.: Inferring high-level behavior from low-level sensors. In: UbiComp 2003: Ubiquitous Computing, pp. 73–89. Springer, Berlin (2003)
16. Ranganathan, A., Al-Muhtadi, J., Campbell, R.H.: Reasoning about uncertain contexts in pervasive computing environments. IEEE Pervasive Comput. **3**(2), 62–70 (2004)
17. Tanenbaum, A.: Computer Networks, 4th edn. Prentice Hall Professional Technical Reference (2002)
18. Want, R., Hopper, A., Falcao, V., Gibbons, J.: The active badge location system. ACM Trans. Inf. Syst. **10**(1), 91–102 (1992)
19. Wishart, R., Henricksen, K., Indulska, J.: Context obfuscation for privacy via ontological descriptions. In: LoCA, pp. 276–288 (2005)

Chapter 7
Sources, Models and Use of Location:
A Special Sort of Context

Location, as a form of context and as a specialised concern, has been a central consideration of pervasive computing from the start. Location, as a way of indexing data and through distribution of computation, has an even more venerable history in computer science. Of particular interest here is the nature of data which describes the world and associates the virtual with the physical world, and so there is some overlap with Geographical Information Systems (GIS). In this chapter we shall review some of the key ideas about location in computing and their application in pervasive computing.

7.1 Uses of Location

Location has many uses in pervasive computing, helping applications understand questions including:

- Where am I?
- Where is v?
- Who is near?
- Is w within 100 m of me?
- Where should I go to find the nearest x?
- Where was I when y happened?
- How do I get to z?

In all cases the identifier z etc. may identify a unique object in the world, e.g. "John" or "my laptop", specify some class of objects, e.g. "colour printer", or describe a pattern to match, e.g. "co-location with Fred" or "open space of 100–200 m^2". The case of "where is v" highlights an interesting pair of subdivisions: Firstly, whether the object being located is the thing or person that is really of interest, or some proxy, e.g. a person's mobile phone. Secondly, whether the object being located is participating in the act of being located, unaware, or being uncooperative. A participating object will be a computational device, possibly enhanced by location awareness hardware, engaging in a protocol to share information. An uncooperative object, often in a military scenario, is actively avoiding detection by blocking signals, camouflaging its presence or providing mis-information. A willing participant may obfuscate their location to manage privacy, which is different to the uncooperative case. An unaware object is neither actively seeking engagement nor hindering observation. It may not yet be aware of some benefit to being located, which may be advertised to it once located; the location of objects may be treated in aggregate, e.g. locating cars in order to identify unoccupied parking spaces; or the located objects may remain unaware of being tracked, e.g. in monitoring animal migration, or resigned to being tracked through some legal obligation, e.g. emergency phone call location or security surveillance. In this book we shall concentrate on those cases where being located allows or enhances engagement with a service.

Location acts both a form of context and as a special sort of data in mobile applications. Our presentation is equally relevant to both interpretations. Our notation of $C_{a,o}$ still fits: the aspect is location, the object is the *located object*; often in context awareness the primary object of interest is ourselves, but with location awareness we are often also interested in the location of other objects as well. Returning to the types of context awareness from Chap. 5, we can find uses of location for each of them:

1. Context display is often manifested as showing a map of the current location.
2. Context aware configuration may use a model of nearby resources to configure a system. "Nearby" might be physically near, such as a local printer, or near in system terms, such as a proxy-server with a good (high bandwidth, low latency, probably few hops) network connection.
3. Context triggered actions might cause behaviour on reaching a particular place (home, my office, the train) or when location changes, e.g. request a new map when current location is half-way to the edge of the old map.
4. Contextual augmentation may annotate records of events with their location, and the co-location of important others.
5. Contextual mediation may modify data depending on location, or distance from destination.
6. Contextual adaptation of the environment may cause heating and lighting preferences to follow a user, locating the responsible controllers for the current location as it changes.
7. Context aware presentation may modify the display of private information depending on the location of the user, and the presence of others.

By considering possible questions and possible uses of context we have already, informally, raised the possibility of relations (within 100 m, nearest), fuzzy relations (near), route finding, interpreting the local features of a location, dynamic location information (who is where, as well as static roads and buildings), semantic locations (home) and coordinates relative to a reference (show on map). Rather than give a series of solutions, in this chapter we shall set out some well-understood tools that are appropriate to devising solutions to these, and other location-based, problems.

7.2 Coordinate Models

Coordinate models are built into some systems, but an outline of the underlying principles seems appropriate here. Many of the ideas in this section are developed in more detail in standard geography / GIS texts and technical documents such as (the rather UK centric) Ordnance Survey model [20] and product manuals.

7.2.1 GIS

Geographic Information Systems (GIS) have been a subject of research and commercial development for many years. The data sets provided are a rich source of information about the world for pervasive computing to tap. GIS systems typically use *vector* map formats, representing individual features with detailed position and semantic information—rather than the *raster* maps we are more familiar with, where the set of features and rendering are pre-determined. Representing individual features and classes of feature allows customised maps to be produced, combining data sets. This rich description can support many location aware applications beyond the map, by making use of rich models of place and sophisticated data descriptions. The description of features can be sub-categorised:

- *Fields* describe the properties of regions in space, mapping from place to property, even where the boundaries are indistinct. This model lends itself to many typical GIS situations, including aerial photographic data sources and continuous systems of geography and environment.
- *Objects* are an alternative to fields, whose concept will be familiar to computer scientists. In GIS an object describes a physical entity, with defined boundaries, which can be represented on a map. Object models lend themselves to situations where legally defined entities, e.g. land ownership are being described, and where mobile assets, e.g. trucks, parcels, are moving against a largely static backdrop.
- Objects may further be defined as *points*, with a single spatial location; *lines* or *curves*, with start and end points and a path between them; or *polygons*, with a boundary defined by a series of points. This basic model is found in many spatial data definitions, although often with extensions, such as: *Collections*, defined as multiples of one of the other types; relationships, e.g. road lines connected by junction points; and additional attributes, including directionality for a line.

OpenGIS[1] is a popular current GIS description standard which embodies many of these characteristics.

Google Maps[2] provides an easily accessed view of combined raster (satellite) and vector drawings (e.g. roads, although may be presented to the browser as pre-drawn

---

[1] http://www.opengeospatial.org/.

[2] http://maps.google.com.

rasters) with other data sets (e.g. images, traffic). Open Street Map[3] also provides map data, in this case open source in XML format, with pre-generated raster tiles of various styles. In both cases an API is provided which is a good basis for projects involving wide-scale located data.

The combination of data sources also introduces various potential problems: Data arising from different survey processes may be produced at different times (creating mis-match where features change), to various scales (implying different accuracy), with different equipment (implying different accuracy and error patterns), using different ontologies to describe common features. Data which are derived from paper maps can also suffer from distortions in the drawing process, designed to make the original data legible, e.g. magnification of roads and slight movement of otherwise overlapping features. The combination can lead to *registration* problems in the combined data set, where features do not align quite as they do on the ground; and where real experience does not quite align to the map data.

The issue of error from Chap. 6 is then raised again: features in the world move; reference systems for describing the world are inaccurate; survey methods have limits on their accuracy and potential for error; systems for describing the conceptual world are varied; and processing of location data can introduce numerical errors.

7.2.2 Points of Reference

Many location systems use coordinates in a flat plane as a reference system to describe location. The plane is an approximation for an area of the earth, which holds true over day-to-day experience within smaller areas, the curvature of the earth being quite gently varying. The mapping of the curved earth to a planar representation is known as a *projection*. The plane makes much of the geometry involved in calculating relationships between points far simpler. However, it should be noted that this is not precise and introduces distortions, depending on the projection used some of: area, shape, direction, bearing, distance and scale become inaccurate to some degree—as illustrated in Fig. 7.1. Note that the final projection, a rectilinear grid is convenient, but only valid as an approximation over relatively small areas. Similarly modelling the earth as a sphere is incorrect when examined in detail (the north-south radius is approximately 21 km shorter than the equatorial radius); an ellipsoid is a better approximation—although there is not simply one choice of ellipsoid as a best fit. The fit is usually determined with reference to the oceans as they have a substantially uniform surface.

Latitude and longitude are used as a reference to position on the spherical or ellipsoidal model, but not exclusively—much location information is described in terms of local grid systems (and most countries or regions have their own approximations which introduce the least error within their own scope), and so transformation is still required.

---

[3]http://www.openstreetmap.org.

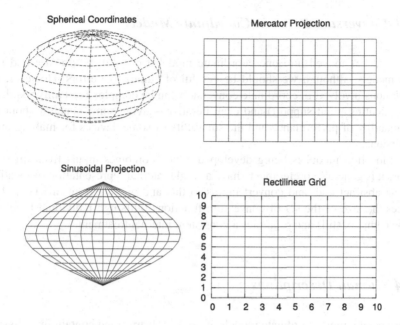

Fig. 7.1 Map projections

For elevation sea level is commonly used as a reference point, but sea level varies with time (due to local volume of water, tides etc.)—so a local mean sea level is usually used. Reference to the centre of gravity, or the intersection of the spin axis and the equatorial plane, might be globally more precise but has (historically at least) been difficult to use in practise. GPS makes a global reference easier to acquire, but elevation is not the most accurate aspect of GPS. Barometric altimeters are still in widespread use (e.g. in aircraft, some cycle computers and GPS units) but are only as accurate as their calibration. To know your height the air pressure at a known elevation is required. To differentiate change in height from change in pressure requires fresh reference data—often from weather stations (landing an aeroplane to check air pressure in order to know your altitude presents a problem!). Radar and sonar methods require knowledge of location and a known reference point to be in range.

It is traditional to align one axis of the grid to the North–South axis. Again, this introduces choices and approximations: The true and magnetic north poles are not exactly aligned and the difference varies over time. The axis of spin also varies in relation to the orbital plane of the earth. The result is that grid coordinates for a known point need to be described with reference to both a projection and a datum for that projection, which describe the interpretation of those coordinates with reference to a current compass reading or stellar reference point.

7.2.3 Conversion Between Coordinate Models

Once data has moved into one coordinate model it can still be transformed into other models, although we should be careful of cumulative errors. However, the calculations involved in coordinate conversion can be complex (certainly requiring proper floating point support) and even iterative—giving some concern about the predictability of performance and the suitability of some devices for making these conversions.

If a location model is being developed which combines inputs from different sensors it is generally preferable to have a single internal representation of location, even an abstract one, and convert inputs to this and outputs from this [15]. This reduces the size of the set of conversion functions (although individual functions can be complex still) and promotes a consistent internal treatment.

7.2.4 Human Descriptions

Unfortunately, most coordinate models are rather abstract and contain few physical manifestations—so human descriptions do not naturally come in the form of grid references. Indeed, even given a reference point most people are not particularly accurate in estimating distance and direction. A more usual spatial description by a person is descriptive:

- A symbolic name, e.g. "my home". Note that this location is with reference to the person making it.
- An address, e.g. The West Pier, Brighton, UK. As databases of addresses are often available this form is most easily translated to a coordinate system.
- With reference to a landmark, e.g. "the tall tower in the middle of town". Note that which "town" is implicit in this example.
- Relative to some known location, e.g. "next door to my office" or "1 km from here along this road".

Variously things which are *adjacent* or *visible from*, things which have a *visible connection* or *relationship*, things which are *labelled* or *match some pattern* and things which are *contained*. A common technique in navigation (in particular in orienteering) is to aim approximately towards a goal with the intention of finding a large or linear feature—this does not require accurate aim or distance measurement. Having found the reference feature, e.g. a track, possibly deliberately *aiming off* to one side, the real target can be found in relation to this. In spatial databases (see [19] for a deeper discussion of this) this generates a requirement that such relationships can be described as search terms. When collecting data in pervasive systems which are indexed by location we should be aware of the need to use that data later and the value of relationships between data as well as absolute positioning of data. However, the literature generally defers to coordinate systems and/or GIS approaches to achieve this. The main departure from this is in some sensor systems where location models are developed by using radio visibility between nodes.

Having established sources of location data and coordinate systems it is necessary to be able to interpret the location. For a map to display "you are here" coordinates are sufficient (indeed, preferred). For more complex behaviours it is the nature of the place, rather than the particular place in the world, that is often of most interest, e.g. being at home, at work, in my office, in your office, in a lecture theatre and so on.

In Leonhardt and Magee [14, 15] inputs which describe the located objects within *cells* are considered; these include an active badge system, UNIX `rusers` login detection, and GPS. Cells naturally describe objects—as discussed there is always an error associated with a location reading, and most objects occupy a measurable volume in space. A cell can be described as disjoint, identical, within, overlapping or adjacent-to another cell. The cells arising from active badge detectors and logins have well defined zones of meaning—the space described is a volume not a point. Cells derived from GPS are regions on a coordinate space, which have a variable size due to reception quality. In general there is a mapping between the various location sources' coordinate systems, via the cells—although only to the granularity of the cell. An illustration of four cells is given in Fig. 7.2. Here cells A and B are disjoint in space, and cells C and D are contained within cell B. Clearly describing all possible GPS locations with all possible accuracies in advance is impractical, so cells are generated dynamically to represent such readings. In this case a mapping from a coordinate space into the higher level model is required. Given the spatial descriptions of locations a hierarchical model of *location domains* is built up: a university containing a campus, containing a building, containing a room etc. Another model of location, which uses a similar semantic map and operator arrangement, is described with a variety of applications in [3].

In using models of the world based on GIS vector data the semantics of the data are given: each feature has a separate data entry, which includes both the coordinates and meta data. Key to the latter is a pointer to a type system or ontology describing the possible kinds of feature. For some data this will be equivalent to a map legend, for others GML and OWL and similar will be used.

7.2.5 Relationships

It is all very well being able to describe individual objects in space, but many of the uses of location context we identified above relied upon being able to describe relative location:

- Who is near?
- Is w within 100 m of me? (which requires finding objects within a scope)
- Where is the nearest x? (which requires measuring distance between objects)
- How do I get to z? (which requires finding a connected path through a series of transport paths)

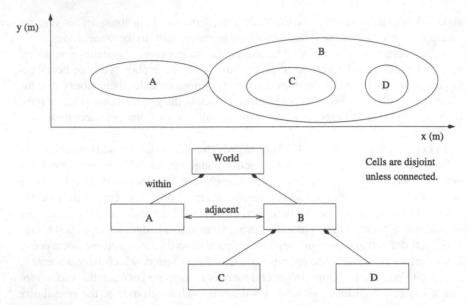

Fig. 7.2 Geometric and symbolic (cell) locations, based on [15]. Ulf Leonhardt and Jeff Magee. Multi-sensor location tracking. In *4th ACM/IEEE Conference on Mobile Computing and Networks (MobiCom)*, pages 203–214. ACM, 1998, http://doi.acm.org/10.1145/288235.288291 © 1998 Association for Computing Machinery, Inc. Reprinted by permission

A useful working model of object comparisons is given in [5] and summarised here and in Fig. 7.3. An object (shown as ellipses, but applicable to any polygon with a boundary) has three zones in space: exterior, boundary (∂) and interior ($\circ$). The intersection of two objects may be considered by comparing each of the zones of each of the objects, or by looking at four spatial relationships: intersecting boundaries ($\partial\partial$), common interiors ($\circ\circ$), boundary as part of interior ($\partial\circ$) and interior as part of boundary ($\circ\partial$), as shown in Table 7.1. This second representation avoids reasoning about the exterior of an object, which can simplify complexity where there are many objects. Each of these four relations can be empty ($\emptyset$) or non-empty ($\neg\emptyset$).

The GIS / spatial database literature, indeed even the cited paper, contains other aspects of relationships which might need to be considered, e.g. whether objects meet at a point or along a length and the handling of relationships between collections where multiple points, or polygons with "holes" in must be considered.

7.2.6 Summary

The processing model for context in Fig. 5.1 remains appropriate here: location data requires sensor processing and a conversion into a low-level model. The low level data can be further processed to give a high level model. Location sources can be fused, at high or low level, to provide greater accuracy or confidence. Location can

Table 7.1 A mathematical model of topological relationships based on [5]

Relation	$\partial\partial$	oo	∂o	o∂
disjoint	$\emptyset$	$\emptyset$	$\emptyset$	$\emptyset$
equal	$\neg\emptyset$	$\neg\emptyset$	$\emptyset$	$\emptyset$
meet	$\neg\emptyset$	$\emptyset$	$\emptyset$	$\emptyset$
contains	$\emptyset$	$\neg\emptyset$	$\emptyset$	$\neg\emptyset$
inside	$\emptyset$	$\neg\emptyset$	$\neg\emptyset$	$\emptyset$
covers	$\neg\emptyset$	$\neg\emptyset$	$\emptyset$	$\neg\emptyset$
covered-by	$\neg\emptyset$	$\neg\emptyset$	$\neg\emptyset$	$\emptyset$
overlaps	$\neg\emptyset$	$\neg\emptyset$	$\neg\emptyset$	$\neg\emptyset$

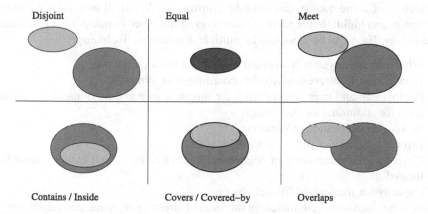

Fig. 7.3 A visual model of topological relationships based on [5]

be described as a state, or that state can be interpreted by an event detector. A similar location stack, with fusion, is also described in many papers, e.g. [10, 15].

In [11] Jiang and Steenkiste discuss coordinate systems, and take the view that neither coordinate models nor semantic models by themselves are satisfactory. They propose a URI system for describing places (volumes) in either, or a mix, of these systems. The mix of description systems also allows for conversion between systems with local, rather than global, points of reference. This is integrated into a database system to provide for efficient searches in a location space (see also below on R-Trees), with the usual spatial relations.

7.3 Sources of Location Data

Location sources can take various forms, but can be classified into two basic forms: those which determine location with respect to global coordinates, using known reference points; and those which simply determine location with respect to other nodes in the system. We shall be concentrating on the first sort here. There are various techniques for calculating the relationship of a node to the nodes which have a known location, which we shall survey below. We focus on those where the reference nodes are easily found, and so are most applicable to general purpose pervasive computing. The more general solutions for fewer known reference points or purely relative location are typically addressed in texts on sensor networks. These various sources have different properties: some require particular antennae, membership of services, certain processing power; some are sensitive to configuration, environmental factors and require up-to-date survey data; some drain power faster than others or provide information faster than others; some are more accurate than others; some describe their data in different ways; each has a range over which it can operate due to the deployment of its associated infrastructure. Between the various systems a location of some quality can often be constructed. We shall now briefly survey the issues and highlight the main choices to examine when considering a particular technology. Each can be classified in multiple dimensions, including:

1. What reference system is required to interpret the location data
2. Whether locations are described as coordinates or symbolic
3. Deployment and maintenance costs for infrastructure and marginal deployment costs for additional located objects
4. Resolution of location information
5. Error characteristics of location information
6. Coverage, including scale of operation and environments that can or cannot be located-in
7. Capacity for tracking additional objects
8. Whether location is computed on the located object or by some central service

You may wish to consider some of these (and possibly other) criteria as you read this, and research more detail on location systems.

7.3.1 Cellular Systems

A primary source of location information is gained through proximity to a sensor. The range of the sensor may vary, but if presence is detected then the located object can be said to be within that sensor's range (or cell). In some cases this requires contact with the sensor: pressure on a seat etc. One removed from this is contact (or other very close connection) with some proxy for the located object, e.g. terminal activity on a computer, and swipe cards on doors as proxies for user location, RFID tags as proxies for object location.

If cells are designed such that there is *no* overlap, then cell ID can translate to a region in a trivial manner. Note that the cell may broadcast its ID, or a device may broadcast a query for location information. In a system where a device will only see or be seen by one reference node (or beacon, base station) there is little difference, apart from any overheads.

As cells become more dense, so that regions usually overlap, the location can become more accurate as the intersection of cells reduces the possible region referred to. If the cells are defined as regions around the known location of reference nodes in a regular grid then the average coordinate in each axis of the reference nodes seen at some point defines the centroid of the device to be located. As the overlap ratio of beacon range to separation increases the average error in this centroid becomes a smaller multiple of the beacon separation [4]. In real world settings the variation in beacon position and range due to the environment means that a regular grid may not be seen, but geometric intersection of known (or expected) signal patterns can still be used to identify a region which contains the device to be located. Where cells overlap there is also a greater possibility of beacons or query responses overlapping, although being static beacon timing may be easier to plan than the response to a query from a device with an unknown location.

Location systems can be derived from ad-hoc sensors. In this category we include cellular systems from 802.11 SSIDs gained by "war-driving" and Bluetooth beacon sensing. We note these as being different as (in the general case) the number of beacons can be of the same order as the number of users; the ownership of beacons is widely dispersed (certainly more than single infrastructure owner or a few mobile phone operators); and because the operation and location of individual beacons is variable. In the case of Bluetooth beacon sensing between mobile phones all that can really be established without further data is that the two devices are co-located within a mobile cell (*cell* as used above not the phone operator's base station derived cell) which just encompasses the two phones by the range of Bluetooth. The Place Lab project[4] [13] uses 802.11 and GSM base-stations as beacons and demonstrates very good coverage in somewhat urban areas and the ability to operate both indoors and out. The paper includes a useful discussion of the trade-offs inherent in designing location systems, in this case some accuracy is lost in allowing easy set-up, good coverage and a real consideration of privacy issues.

7.3.2 Multi-Reference Point Systems

Some location systems require inputs from multiple sources in order to arrive at a location, by *triangulation* or *trilateration* e.g. GPS, ultrasonic systems with a mesh of sensors in the room, use of signal strength from multiple wireless network basestations etc. Here geometry is applied so that multiple distance (trilateration) or angle measurements (triangulation) from beacons which do not map into a single plane are combined to find the place of intersection. In general using distance measurements requires (at least) $D + 1$ measurements, i.e. 3 measurements for 2D, 4 measurements for 3D. Where the system implies extra information about the relative location of object of interest and transmitters is known this number can be reduced, e.g. in GPS satellites are above the receiver. Using angular measurements is similar,

---

[4]http://www.placelab.org.

but the distance separating two sources is usually required; sometimes a constant reference such as magnetic north is used. In both cases installation specific knowledge can be applied to simplify the problem. Distance is rarely measured directly, with a tape measure, but through other measures such as time of flight and signal attenuation. These measures can sometimes be had with little cost due to existing infrastructure, e.g. 802.11 base stations, but can require calibration to the local environment. Time of flight either requires precisely synchronised clocks (rather hard to achieve in practise); or two signals, commonly RF and audio, so that time of flight is determined from the difference. Over large scales Vincenty's formula should be applied for calculating distance on an ellipsoid.

We shall not discuss all triangulation systems here, although examples of ultrasonic, wireless LAN, cellular phone network, wireless with purpose designed infrastructure and others can be found in the literature. By way of example we shall give a brief review of one of the most common triangulation systems: the Global Positioning System (GPS).

7.3.2.1 Global Positioning System

GPS is a US military system for providing location through measuring delay (and hence distance) from multiple satellites—a form of trilateration. While it was deployed as a joint-forces project it has been made available for civilian use as a common good. It uses highly accurate atomic clocks on satellites to transmit a time signal, which also send data on their orbits ("ephemeris") to allow calculation of time of flight and approximate data on other satellite positions to aid signal acquisition ("almanac"). At least four satellites must be visible to achieve an accurate 3D location plus time, from a constellation of at least 24 satellites in medium Earth orbit. This orbit means that each satellite moves across the sky when seen from a stationary point on the Earth's surface, requiring a receiver to scan for new signals but providing robustness against individual satellite failure and ensuring satellites are distributed across the sky to facilitate global coverage and accuracy.

A message from an individual satellite is encoded using Code Division Multiple Access (CDMA), allowing all satellites to share a frequency band. This message is decoded and arrival time recorded using an internal clock at the receiver. This clock is not synchronised with the satellite clock, so cannot by itself compute a distance. However, the difference in time of flight between satellites together with ephemeris can be used to compute an initial distance estimate. Due to the very short times small timing errors imply large positioning errors and the distance calculation must include corrections for relativistic effects. This distance describes a sphere in space centred on the satellite (although it is assumed the receiver is below the orbit, so a full sphere is not required). As additional satellite signals are decoded additional spheres can be described. Receiver position is computed from the intersection of the spheres. This requires that the satellites are not lying on the same plane as each other; but their number and orbits help to ensure this condition is met. A fourth satellite signal is usually used to correct the GPS receiver's internal clock,

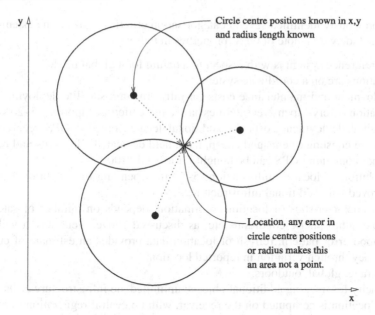

Circle centre positions known in x,y
and radius length known

Location, any error in
circle centre positions
or radius makes this
an area not a point.

Fig. 7.4 A 2D illustration of lateration, with circles of known centre and radius

by measuring the distance from it's sphere to the 3-satellite position estimate. With an accurate clock a new estimate of time of flight, and hence distance to satellite, can be produced. This computation is typically an iterative estimation, improving the local clock accuracy and acquiring additional signals to refine the accuracy of the distance estimates and hence reducing the error in the position estimate. During initial signal acquisition movement makes this refinement of timing rather difficult and leads to delays in achieving an accurate estimate of location. The principle of lateration used in GPS is illustrated in Fig. 7.4.

There is some inherent uncertainty in GPS data, arising from various factors including:

- Satellite clock accuracy causing drift over time, this is frequently updated.
- Accuracy of the measured signal delay limiting resolution.
- Accuracy of the model of real satellite position for calculating signal delay, this is frequently updated.
- Atmospheric variation, which is the least easy to model and predict the effect on signal time of flight.
- Selective availability, introducing deliberate errors of up to 100 m into the signal for military purposes, can be corrected for using differential GPS.

This is not the only satellite based positioning system, but it is the most widely known and GPS receivers are easily available consumer products, built into many smart-phones and other devices. The most obvious alternative system is the EU "Galileo" system whose satellites are currently being deployed.

We previously identified several categorisation criteria for location systems. We shall conclude with a note of GPS' properties in these:

1. The reference system is with respect to a datum for a global model.
2. Locations are on a coordinate system.
3. Deployment and maintenance costs for infrastructure: satellite deployment and operation is very expensive; satellites have a finite lifetime (approx. 15–20 years). Marginal deployment costs for additional located objects: GPS receiver circuits are consumer items and cheap, hand-held dedicated GPS units and mobile phones containing GPS can be bought for around £100.
4. Resolution of location information: 5–50 m depending on conditions, can be improved with additional infrastructure.
5. Error characteristics of location information: depends on number of satellites visible, atmospheric conditions etc. as discussed above. Generally a well understood error pattern, refresh of location data provides an estimate of current accuracy through variation in reported location.
6. Coverage: global, outdoors.
7. Capacity for tracking additional objects: unlimited, no infrastructure costs.
8. The location is computed on the receiver, with no central registration or awareness of connection.

7.3.3 Tagging

Systems with *tags* allow location to be determined in two ways:

- By fixing tags at known locations, when a tag is scanned the scanner must be within scanning range (which depends on the technology) of the tag's location.
- By having tags report to some infrastructure cellular or triangulation techniques can be applied.

The latter approach featured in the active badge project [21] and is effectively a variation on the schemes elsewhere in this chapter. In this section we shall discuss the first case—where scanning a tag generates a location event describing proximity to the tag. This type of tagging is common in what is known as "the Internet of Things", where everyday objects have an internet presence (typically a web presence), which is sometimes deployed in a manner overlapping with augmented reality. In some cases this presence will be achieved by embedding computation and networking into the object in other cases there will simply be a presence about the object on the web. In either situation, it is common to "tag" objects to facilitate identification of their address in the internet, and visual tags can facilitate user-identification of objects of interest. We can further consider five classifications axes of this approach:

1. The "location" of the tag may be fixed, e.g. tags to identify rooms, bus stops etc., or the tag may be attached to a mobile object, in which case the location *only* describes proximity rather than absolute position.

2. The tags may be unique, e.g. Bluetooth tags with a MAC address, the tag may have duplicates, e.g. identifying a shop by brand not location, or a given location may have multiple tags, e.g. at different entrances or identifying different properties of the place. Where tags are intended to be unique one should consider whether security or functionality issues arise from forgery or accidental reuse or tag re-positioning.
3. The range that a reader can read a tag over. This may be variable for a given technology, influenced by tag and reader design, available power, and the environment.
4. The cost and integration involved in deploying the tags and the cost and integration involved in reading tags. There may be set-up costs for a system where tags refer to an infrastructure.
5. The behaviour mode of the tag—reader system, including: whether the reading of a tag is automatic or manually triggered; and whether the reading is an entry or trigger event or a presence state.

The first classification is generally a property of deployment rather than technology, as the usual model is that the marginal costs for tags is very low (often to the point of being disposable) and the maintenance of tags is very low (often ruling out powered tags). This cost model is an important property for the Internet of Things model (and pervasive computing generally), where everyday objects would acquire a tag and so quantities of tags are very large compared to quantities of readers, and the functionality tends to be concentrated towards the user rather than the environment. There are various systems which can function in this way, we shall briefly examine three which give rise to systems with different properties: Bluetooth, RFID and QR codes.

7.3.3.1 Bluetooth

Bluetooth enabled devices can be used as a form of tagging. To act as a tag a device needs to have its Bluetooth switched on and discoverable. To act as a reader a device needs to scan for other Bluetooth devices. The tag data can simply be the tag's unique Bluetooth address, which tells the reader little about the device but is easy to acquire and could be correlated with other data. In this case the tag is not aware of the reader detecting it and where tags are in fact personal devices (quite common) it may give rise to privacy concerns—particularly where the device has been given a personal name, or where the readers store scans and correlate with other data (a network of readers in other locations, very particular reader locations, video observations etc.). Intrusive observation can be defeated by making personal devices not-discoverable, except when pairing and by limiting correlation of reading events with other data.

In terms of our four distinguishing properties:

1. The tags are generally unique, but a given location may have multiple tags.

2. The range depends on power and antenna design for both reader and tag. A typical configuration would allow detection over 5–10 m, although longer range devices may extend this and substantial walls and metal structures may reduce it.
3. Bluetooth circuits are built into many consumer devices, where these already exist the cost approaches zero. The cost for additional tags is low. The energy cost of tag beacons and reader scanning can be quite high, cf mobile phone battery life with Bluetooth on.
4. Once switched on and properly coded the scanning can be automatic, frequent, registers presence and is invisible to the human observer—although each of these properties can be modified in code and/or device configuration.

7.3.3.2 Radio Frequency ID

Radio Frequency ID (RFID) tags are widely used in warehouse, retail, library and transport situations, supporting theft detection, stock identification and tracking and account identity for payment. Reading is contact-less, using radio (unlike a smartcard), with range depending on available power and antenna design—typically a few cm to a metre. A tag consists of an aerial and some small memory and/or computing capacity plus two-way radio interface circuitry, typically printed on a label or embedded in a card. A wide range of radio frequencies and protocols (some standard, some proprietary) are in use, with choice affecting tag and reader size, power consumption, range and data transfer speed. Different systems also have differing abilities to handle reading multiple in-range tags at once. The tag and aerial are often several cm across, but miniaturisation is progressing, antenna design for a desired range being a limiting factor. It is possible to embed a power source into a tag, but we will focus on the more common (for this application domain) passive-RFID, where power is extracted from the radio signal of the reader in order to power the tag while it is being read. A few mobile phones have built-in readers, but in general the hardware is special-purpose. The tag data depends on the design of the tag, and can range from a simple numeric ID (used in a similar way to a bar-code for stock control), to more complex structured records. The tag computation may range from unauthenticated, un-encrypted data exchange on demand, to protocols which require an identifier and provide simple encryption; some protocols may also record tag reading events or cause tag data to be changed. The modification of tag data increases the need for security provision but allows the tag system to function where access to a database indexed by tag data is problematic. The main barrier to invisible tag reading is the need to camouflage long range antennas, and as possession of tagged objects could reveal quite personal data their use has been somewhat limited.

1. The tags may be unique where suitable security provisions have been made but for simpler technology should be treated as duplicatable, a given location may have multiple tags and it may be possible to read them all in one scan.
2. Tag range is from mm to a few meters, generally requiring clear air.
3. The marginal cost of a tag is very low and they are widely used as disposable labels for low value goods. The costs of tag producing / writing hardware is higher.

Reader costs are moderate, often requiring integration with other systems. Power costs of reading are significant, but passive RFID has no routine maintenance cost.

4. Once switched on and properly coded the scanning is automatic, frequent, registers presence and is invisible to the human observer. Modifying this behaviour is hard as the tags and scanner are less likely to be easily user programmable and incorporate displays than in the Bluetooth case.

7.3.3.3 Bar Codes

Bar codes are commonly found on printed product packaging, and provide a simple optical ID system. We shall focus on 2D matrix bar codes, in particular QR codes[5] here as these are widely used and easily read with mobile phone cameras. The tag can encode numbers, alphanumeric codes, 8-bit binary or kanji, the typical internet-of-things approach would be to encode a URL, but the data is arbitrary. The code can be read from any angle, is somewhat damage resistant, and the detail required depends on the amount of data being encoded—so short URLs are preferred. To deploy codes requires some software to encode the data into a black and white image (widely and freely available) and a printer or display. To read the code requires a simple camera (mobile phone cameras are ample) and software—again, widely available and increasingly supplied with the phone. The reading of such a code is a one way process, the tag being unaware unless it is displayed by a device which is informed of any data access triggered by the encoded data. Lighting conditions (bright lights and darkness) can interfere with tag reading, particularly with glossy weatherproofing. Unless a camera is concealed the act of reading a tag is generally visible.

1. The tags are easily duplicated and a given location may have multiple tags, if there is space to display them.
2. The range depends on lighting, printer size and camera quality, but is usually under a metre in practical applications.
3. Cameras are built into many consumer devices, where these already exist the cost of reading approaches zero. The monetary and power cost for additional tags is low for printed tags, higher for active displays.
4. Reading a tag is typically manually triggered, as the device often has other purposes and required re-enabling after a read, but this behaviour could be changed. The reading of a tag is typically an event.

7.3.4 Fingerprints and Scenes

A final location system we shall mention only briefly is where locations are recognised through reference to a database of previously surveyed features. Commercial

---

[5]http://www.denso-wave.com/qrcode/index-e.html.

and free systems are available which use this technique, in particular with 802.11 wireless networks. Network base stations can be used to develop a cellular system, where cells are defined by the coverage of a base station. As wireless networks have become more widely deployed it is easy to find that multiple base stations are "seen". If the location of each base station is known then the centroid of these can give an approximation to the receiver's location. If the networks are operating in an open space then trilateration based on received signal strength can be used to find the location. However, for the general case trilateration is problematic as antenna properties may vary and obstacles cause complex changes to signal propagation. It is in this situation that fingerprinting is used.

A survey is made of the space to be covered, by recording received base station identifiers and, ideally, signal strengths and correlating these with some external location system, typically manual registration on a map or by using GPS. This process can occur with high resolution, e.g. on a 1 m grid in an office space, e.g. Ekahau[6] or by driving through a built-up area, e.g. [13]. For high resolution signal strength is required, and it may be necessary to take readings for a given point with people in different places relative to the receiver aerial to form a reliable model. For all uses periodic re-surveying is required as objects which affect signal propagation change and deployment of base stations changes (through user switching at different times of day, renaming, replacement and addition / removal). To use the system to locate an object at a later date the wireless network is scanned and base station IDs and signal strengths used to query a database. The database will report a best match taking account of noise and variation models, possibly interpolating between reference points.

Related to this technique is *scene analysis*, which is a visual technique but also operates by comparing a reading of the location with a database of previously recorded data. Here photographs are used to build models of prominent features in a located database. To use the system to locate an object a photograph is taken. The picture is analysed for key features, e.g. buildings, hills etc. These are then compared to the database, taking into account changes due to camera lens (and so distortions and relative sizes of features) and angle of view. Even for a restricted coverage this is a complex visual search, but the subject of research in image analysis and information retrieval communities.

7.3.5 Summary

As we have seen, there are many ways to compute location and an even greater number of technologies applying these principles. Different technologies give different trade-offs in the classification we gave at the start of this section. We shall now review these categories, noting systems which occupy various places in it.

---

[6]http://www.ekahau.com/.

1. Many systems, including GPS and Place Lab, use a global *reference system*. The Active Badge system describes a location relative to a smaller coordinate space, defined by the system coverage.
2. *Coordinate* systems include GPS and within-room positioning systems. *Symbolic* locations are given by most tagging systems. Other systems, such as fingerprinting and cellular systems may be designed to use either approach.
3. As discussed above deployment and maintenance *costs* for GPS infrastructure is large, while QR-code tagging can be very cheap. Costs associated with locating an object are often absorbed into other aspects of the system, such as wireless networks and cameras in mobile phones.
4. *Resolution* varies from sub-cm for some RFID (although limited to proximity to a tag), through 0.1 to 5 m for many indoor systems; to 5 to 50 m for GPS and <150 to <300 m for different forms of E911 legislated phone location.
5. *Error characteristics* of location information are generally very complex. The simplest are defined as ranges around tagging systems. Stability of any infrastructure is a significant factor.
6. GPS gives global *coverage* but requires something close to out-of-doors with clear sky on the Earth; ultrasonics require in-building infrastructure and only operate within rooms where the infrastructure is deployed. Tags create cells of location coverage.
7. Capacity for tracking *additional objects* is very high in many of these systems, but cellular systems are generally limited by base station capacity. The willingness of owners to allow objects to be tagged (and physical space) limits QR codes' capacity for located objects.
8. Most of the systems we have examined compute location at the receiver, as this simplifies reliability and scalability; the active badge and use of any central reference databases in tagging systems and fingerprinting are obvious exceptions. Privacy should be considered separately as once computed it is easy to reveal location information through an application even if it is computed locally.

High resolution, global, indoor and outdoor, scalable, reliable and cheap coverage has not yet been achieved. To obtain even reliable, global coverage requires a system which can combine location data from different sources—converting between reference and coordinate systems and adapting to varying resolution, error characteristics. Where the object to be located is covered by multiple location systems at once, the data from these systems can still usefully be combined. Depending on the reference and coordinate systems we may achieve some of:

- Better reliability
- Greater accuracy and/or reduction of error estimates
- Greater flexibility to use either coordinate or symbolic locations

The needs of the system at hand are, as ever, crucial in selecting a trade-off between these factors and the modes of use required.

Having obtained this data it will typically be used to support location awareness in applications. In most cases this implies that data is stored with a location index. This is the subject of the next section.

7.4 Storing and Searching Location Data

Storage of data for efficient look-up using a coordinate data type requires data structures optimised for this sort of use—which is not necessarily the same as for more traditional numeric data types. As discussed in Sect. 7.2 we must consider: multi-dimensional (2 or 3-D) data, relations other than ==, >, < and data which may occupy a space rather than a single value. However, if we consider the storage as a database, then usual drivers remain present: efficient selection queries, insertion and index update; and joins with other data. When using spatial data algorithms and structures which allow approximations to quickly limit the set of data of interest, and focus the more complex computation around these operations on a limited data set—in the same way that e.g. B-tree indices are used for other data types.

In this section we give a brief overview of R-Trees and spatial relations, which tackle the main issues and are the basis of many of the techniques in mainstream use.

7.4.1 R-Trees

A data structure which is widely used in processing geographic data is the R-Tree [7], and its variants, e.g. R*-tree [2]. An R-Tree is a tree data structure which uses location to organise grouping of data within nodes and the relationships between parent and child nodes. Each tree node contains data for a region in space, known as a *bounding box* (we shall describe a 2D model here with rectangular boxes, but n-dimensions are possible). The bounding box minimally contains all the located records in a leaf node or all the child bounding boxes in a non-leaf node. The bounding box for a node may overlap with the bounding boxes for other nodes. The bounding box is a minimal description, so that addition of new data can change the bounding box for a given node. Nodes have a bounded capacity for data items (a configuration parameter), so the tree grows by node division where the algorithm for selecting which sub-tree a data item goes into is a crucial factor in the efficiency of the tree. This bounding capacity is both a minimum and a maximum number of records (except the root). For non-leaf nodes these records will be children; for leaf nodes these records will be data points. The root may either be a leaf or a non-leaf node, in the latter case it will have at least two and at most the maximum capacity of child nodes. See Fig. 7.5 for an example—note that the whole possible space does not need to be under any tree node, that actual data items are only held at the leaf nodes, and that nodes do not need to fill their capacity for data items. We also see that the R-Tree is depth-balanced, so that search complexity is uniform, rather than developing hot-spots—all leaf nodes are on the same level.

The R-Tree algorithm is summarised in Listings 7.1 (insertion basics), 7.2 (search), and 7.3 (tree growth) as an explanation—for implementation refer to the detailed presentation in the paper for the R-Tree [7] or one of its variants. We see that the R-Tree structure lends itself to top-down recursive processing. Some detail is omitted, but the general process for most R-Tree variants is illustrated: find the

Fig. 7.5 An example R-tree
based on [7]. Antonin
Guttman. R-trees: A dynamic
index structure for spatial
searching. In Beatrice
Yormark, editor, *SIGMOD
Conference*, pages 47–57.
ACM Press, 1984,
http://doi.acm.org/10.1145/
971697.602266 © 1984
Association for Computing
Machinery, Inc. Reprinted by
permission

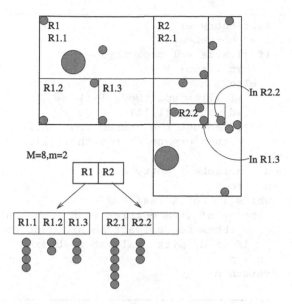

most suitable sub-tree for insertion; manage node size; split nodes if necessary. The
insertion of data is where most of the possible optimisations are to be found—even
the original paper considers three algorithms here. Particular variants of the algorithm have been constructed to improve efficiency for particular circumstances, e.g.
static data sets, highly dynamic data sets, and various underlying storage architectures.

Searches across the resulting data structure are driven by data contained in the
tree, not by an arbitrary organisation of the space; the index is dynamic and doesn't
require periodic rebuilding or any domain knowledge to define. Because nodes may
have overlapping bounding boxes a search may visit multiple leaves.

7.4.2 Spatial Relations

Spatial relations are discussed in many papers on location models, including [3, 11,
15, 17, 18]. R-Trees explicitly focus on a *containment* (or *within*) relation: finding
located objects contained within a region. Some of the other relations which consis-
tently appear in the literature include:

1. Overlaps: where two regions intersect. Containment can be viewed as a special
   case of overlaps, but really has different implications. Overlaps can be described
   as a Boolean, or can give a degree—which describes the proportion of one region
   which overlaps the other.
2. Adjacent, which can be described as two regions which just meet without sharing
   any space.
3. Disjoint: where two regions neither intersect nor are adjacent.

```
insert(Entry e)
  l = chooseLeaf(e)
  if (l.size < l.capacity)
    then l.add(e)
    else
      (l,ll) = splitNode(l,e)
      adjustTree(l,ll)
      if adjustTree caused root split
        then create root with (l,ll) as entries

Node chooseLeaf(Entry e)
  n = root
  while (n not a leaf)
    choose n' from entries in n such that:
      n'.bbox needs least enlargement to include e
      if tied, pick smallest n'.bbox
    n = n'
  return n
}
```

Listing 7.1 The R-tree insert algorithm: basics, based on [7]

```
Entry[] search(Rectangle s)
  n = root
  result = []
  while (n not a leaf)
    for all children c in n
      if overlaps(c.bbox,s)
        then result += search c
  // n is a leaf
  for all entries e in n
    if overlaps(e.bbox,s)
      then result += e
  return result
```

Listing 7.2 The R-tree search algorithm, based on [7]

4. Near or close, which are commonly used without qualification in natural language, allowing nearness to be interpreted relative to size and/or speed; and possibly to have a degree of nearness (relating distance to size and/or speed).
5. Distance describes the separation between two regions. Different interpretations exist, describing maximum, minimum, separation of centres or some combination of these.
6. Relative size similarly compares the areas of two regions.
7. Connected, where there is a path from one region to another through a series of other located objects in the space which overlap or are adjacent to each other in

```
adjustTree(Node l, Node ll)
  while (l != root)
    update bbox entry for l in l.parent
    if (ll != null) // split occurred
      then if (l.parent.size < l.parent.capacity)
        then create entry in l.parent for ll
          // pointer to ll + bbox for ll
        l = l.parent, ll = null
      else (l,ll) = splitNode (l.parent, ll)
    else l = l.parent, ll = null

(Node,Node) splitNode(Node l, Entry e)
  n1, n2 = new Node
  (s1, s2) = pickSeeds(l)
  n1.add(s1), n2.add(s2)
  l.remove(s1), l.remove(s2)
  for each e' in l.entries + e
    if just one of n.size < n.minSize
      then assign remaining entries to n; break
    add e' to n1 or n2 such that:
      n.bbox needs least enlargement to include e'
      if tied pick the smallest n.bbox
      if tied pick the smallest n.size
      if tied pick either
  return (n1,n2)

(Node,Node) pickSeeds(Node l)
  in each dimension find e in l whose bbox have:
    highest low side, lowest high side,
    highest high side, lowest low side
    sep = highest low side - lowest high side
    size = highest high side - lowest low side
    norm_sep[dim] = sep / size
  return entry pair with largest norm_sep
```

Listing 7.3 The R-tree insert algorithm: tree growth, based on [7]

a chain. It may be desirable to constrain the semantics of the features forming such a chain, e.g. to road.

7.5 Summary

As with other forms of context, we should strive to understand the behaviour of the data we are working with, its true meaning (and how this may differ from its apparent meaning), and its error modes. With location sensing the state of the art is well developed: sensor systems are varied and widely deployed; data are available to describe the world in great detail, both conceptually and positionally; algorithms to manipulate sensor data and existing information are mature. Despite this, location remains a subject of active research: new sensors continue to be devised; greater accuracy and efficiency are desired; lower cost and power consumption are required for truly pervasive deployment; and the problem of human meaning and human needs and behaviour is highly complex.

7.6 Suggested Readings

In this chapter we have covered and expanded upon several topics. You may wish to choose readings from several of the following topics, or to pick one and explore more deeply.

On GIS and the management of spatial data:

- Shashi Shekhar and Sanjay Chawla. *Spatial Databases—A Tour*. Pearson Education, Prentice Hall, 2003

  On location sensing:

- Jeffrey Hightower and Gaetano Borriello. Location systems for ubiquitous computing. *IEEE Computer*, 34(8):57–66, 2001 (and also the extended technical report UW-CSE 01-08-03).
- Eamonn O'Neill, Vassilis Kostakos, Tim Kindberg, Ava Fatah gen. Schieck, Alan Penn, Danae Stanton Fraser, and Tim Jones. Instrumenting the city: Developing methods for observing and understanding the digital cityscape. In Paul Dourish and Adrian Friday, editors, *Ubicomp*, volume 4206 of *Lecture Notes in Computer Science*, pages 315–332. Springer, 2006
- Anthony LaMarca, Yatin Chawathe, Sunny Consolvo, Jeffrey Hightower, Ian E. Smith, James Scott, Timothy Sohn, James Howard, Jeff Hughes, Fred Potter, Jason Tabert, Pauline Powledge, Gaetano Borriello, and Bill N. Schilit. Place lab: Device positioning using radio beacons in the wild. In Hans-Werner Gellersen, Roy Want, and Albrecht Schmidt, editors, *Pervasive*, volume 3468 of *Lecture Notes in Computer Science*, pages 116–133. Springer, 2005

A special issue on labelling the world in IEEE Pervasive Computing magazine provides a range of approaches to tying location to places Tim Kindberg, Thomas Pederson, and Rahul Sukthankar. Guest editors' introduction: Labeling the world. *IEEE Pervasive Computing*, 9(2):8–10, 2010

On location models:

- Ulf Leonhardt and Jeff Magee. Towards a general location service for mobile environments. In *Third IEEE Workshop on Services in Distributed and Networked Environments*, pages 43–50. IEEE, 1996
- Changhao Jiang and Peter Steenkiste. A hybrid location model with a computable location identifier for ubiquitous computing. In Gaetano Borriello and Lars Erik Holmquist, editors, *Ubicomp*, volume 2498 of *Lecture Notes in Computer Science*, pages 246–263. Springer, 2002

- Christian Becker and Frank Dürr. On location models for ubiquitous computing. *Personal and Ubiquitous Computing*, 9(1):20–31, 2005

On R-Trees and R^*-Trees:

- Antonin Guttman. R-trees: A dynamic index structure for spatial searching. In Beatrice Yormark, editor, *SIGMOD Conference*, pages 47–57. ACM Press, 1984
- Norbert Beckmann, Hans-Peter Kriegel, Ralf Schneider, and Bernhard Seeger. The R^*-Tree: An efficient and robust access method for points and rectangles. In Hector Garcia-Molina and H. V. Jagadish, editors, *SIGMOD Conference*, pages 322–331. ACM Press, 1990

On applications of location information:

- Roy Want, Andy Hopper, Veronica Falcao, and Jonathan Gibbons. The active badge location system. *ACM Transactions on Information Systems*, 10(1):91–102, 1992
- Michael Beigl, Tobias Zimmer, and Christian Decker. A location model for communicating and processing of context. *Personal and Ubiquitous Computing*, 6(5/6):341–357, 2002

On error in location data and models:

- Ulf Leonhardt and Jeff Magee. Multi-sensor location tracking. In *4th ACM/IEEE Conference on Mobile Computing and Networks (MobiCom)*, pages 203–214. ACM, 1998
- A. Ranganathan and R.H. Campbell. A middleware for context-aware agents in ubiquitous computing environments. In *Middleware*, pages 143–161, 2003
- Dieter Fox, Jeffrey Hightower, Lin Liao, Dirk Schulz, and Gaetano Borriello. Bayesian filtering for location estimation. *IEEE Pervasive Computing*, 2(3):24–33, 2003
- Jeffrey Hightower and Gaetano Borriello. Particle filters for location estimation in ubiquitous computing: A case study. In *UbiComp 2004: Ubiquitous Computing*, pages 88–106. Springer, 2004

7.7 Laboratory Exercises: Process and Store Location Data

The intention of this lab is to explore the processing of sensor data which reveals location information and to examine the use of R-Trees.

1. Identify a source of location data: GPS logs or way-marks; network-location traces, e.g. from Crawdad[7]; or even a distributed collection of person detection from a system as described in lab 8.7. You may need to perform some parsing and define data structures, or to use 3rd party tools and libraries for this.

---

[7]http://crawdad.cs.dartmouth.edu.

2. Process the tracks into an R-Tree implementation (start with the basic version). Again, you may wish to develop the code yourself from the algorithm or use a 3rd party source. Identify places stopped at and tracks / events.

3. Consider the efficiency of algorithms used in either log processing (as if real time) or R-Tree use: both CPU load and memory use matter in pervasive computing. Processing costs vary with algorithms and data structures used. In Listing 7.1 we present the linear cost algorithm for R-Tree insertion from [7], but you may wish to explore algorithms or R-Tree variants. The insertion cost and query costs over the resulting tree vary between algorithms, but also between data access patterns. Which solutions have which properties; do the properties hold across data sets of differing character?

7.8 Laboratory Exercises: Beacons and Location

The intention of this lab is to explore the use of beacons in forming location information. More sophisticated projects in this area might be easier to build using Place-Lab or other existing systems, but here we tackle the underlying issues of collecting data from beacons and interpreting it. We assume the use of the *BlueCove* Bluetooth stack and API here, as this is a free, Apache licensed, cross-platform, Java implementation. The principles are applicable to other implementations. This lab requires that Bluetooth devices are available: on a computer for running programs and some other nearby devices to act as beacons. There is no need for data exchange between these devices, but people with Bluetooth enabled around the working area should be informed so that they can check their security arrangements.

1. Download the BlueCove JAR[8] and open the API documentation[9].

2. Use the `RemoteDeviceDiscovery` example class from the API documentation as a basis, copy this to your development environment, add the JAR to the classpath and test. You should find a list of devices in the area.

3. Modify the code to provide (and possibly store) a scan at a set interval or on a prompt. Move about the area (maybe 4 m at a time initially) and form a map of which devices are visible where. Depending on the space and number of devices you may wish to extend the code to allow systematic mapping.

4. Review the data collected. Which areas in the space can be distinguished? Is a smaller distance between scans needed (to make more sense of data or to better reflect the space)?

5. Repeat the mapping and compare the two sets of data. Have any of the devices seen moved or vanished? Could the identity of these be predicted? For the remaining devices does the mapping show similar results?

6. As an extension to this it would be interesting to form a system which describes a statistical belief about location based on a database of survey results.

---

[8]http://code.google.com/p/bluecove.

[9]http://www.bluecove.org/apidocs.

7. Another extension would be to connect to specific types of beacons which describe their location. This could be achieved using GPS devices providing location data over Bluetooth in a space where GPS works; or by defining a Bluetooth service which gives some self-defined location description. The ability to infer the location of the client from the beacons' locations is interesting to study: certainly there may be separation between the beacon and client (many Bluetooth devices claim a 10 m range) but multiple readings may reduce this uncertainty.

7.9 Laboratory Exercises: Smart-Phone Location

If you are interested in the use of location data in practical scenarios, this lab integrates several concepts fro this chapter. Many smart-phones now integrate GPS receivers, QR code readers and the ability to run user code. The Android platform is a good starting point as the tool-set is free and quite simple to learn for those with the Java background assumed by this book and emulators are available. Working with a smart-phone platform is also good experience in working within the constraints of battery and store.

The specification here is quite general, and depending on your programme of study might be used as a larger scale project.

1. Access location data from your smart-phone, to show current location.
2. Pass your location data stream into one of the error modelling and filtering algorithms from Chap. 6. For some platforms, e.g. Android, the location data may come from GPS or cellular data and so have varying error patterns. Add to this a liveness detector, to identify when the data is old.
3. Report locations with accuracy data to a server and store or plot. Consider that the network may degrade at the same time as GPS signal degrades, e.g. in a tunnel and provide some local store in these situations.
4. Develop a set of behaviours to arise from specified locations. You may wish to match location to specific "points" and to more general areas. For the purposes of the lab these behaviours might simply be printing a message.
5. Consider how you would map from GPS coordinates to a higher level location scheme, such as place names. Consider whether place names might include user-specific places that map onto common conceptual places, e.g. home, work.
6. Consider how your behaviour specifications might work with the rest of the system, for instance: A hierarchical place name system might allow different levels of error to identify different places. In a space where there are no fine-grained specifications nearby is switching the GPS off to save energy a reasonable strategy?
7. Identify situations where the error is large or liveness poor and seek alternative input, such as QR code tags or user input. Consider that these may refer to a different coordinate scheme to the usual location model.
8. If you have other sensor data, such as an accelerometer, available consider whether this can inform your model of error and/or time-out of liveness.

References

1. Becker, C., Dürr, F.: On location models for ubiquitous computing. Pers. Ubiquitous Comput. **9**(1), 20–31 (2005)
2. Beckmann, N., Kriegel, H.-P., Schneider, R., Seeger, B.: The R*-Tree: an efficient and robust access method for points and rectangles. In: Garcia-Molina, H., Jagadish, H.V. (eds.) SIG-MOD Conference, pp. 322–331. ACM Press, New York (1990)
3. Beigl, M., Zimmer, T., Decker, C.: A location model for communicating and processing of context. Pers. Ubiquitous Comput. **6**(5/6), 341–357 (2002)
4. Bulusu, N., Heidemann, J., Estrin, D.: Gps-less low-cost outdoor localization for very small devices. IEEE Pers. Commun. **7**(5), 28–34 (2000) [see also IEEE Wireless Communications]
5. Egenhofer, M.J., Herring, J.R.: A mathematical framework for the definition of topological relationships. In: Brassel, K., Kishimoto, H. (eds.) 4th International Symposium on Spatial Data Handling, pp. 803–813. International Geographical Union, Zurich (1990)
6. Fox, D., Hightower, J., Liao, L., Schulz, D., Borriello, G.: Bayesian filtering for location estimation. IEEE Pervasive Comput. **2**(3), 24–33 (2003)
7. Guttman, A.: R-trees: a dynamic index structure for spatial searching. In: Yormark, B. (ed.) SIGMOD Conference, pp. 47–57. ACM Press, New York (1984)
8. Hightower, J., Borriello, G.: Location systems for ubiquitous computing. IEEE Comput. **34**(8), 57–66 (2001)
9. Hightower, J., Borriello, G.: Particle filters for location estimation in ubiquitous computing: a case study. In: UbiComp 2004: Ubiquitous Computing, pp. 88–106. Springer, Berlin (2004)
10. Hightower, J., Brumitt, B., Borriello, G.: The location stack: a layered model for location in ubiquitous computing. In: WMCSA, p. 22. IEEE Computer Society, Washington (2002)
11. Jiang, C., Steenkiste, P.: A hybrid location model with a computable location identifier for ubiquitous computing. In: Borriello, G., Holmquist, L.E. (eds.) Ubicomp. Lecture Notes in Computer Science, vol. 2498, pp. 246–263. Springer, Berlin (2002)
12. Kindberg, T., Pederson, T., Sukthankar, R.: Guest editors' introduction: labeling the world. IEEE Pervasive Comput. **9**(2), 8–10 (2010)
13. LaMarca, A., Chawathe, Y., Consolvo, S., Hightower, J., Smith, I.E., Scott, J., Sohn, T., Howard, J., Hughes, J., Potter, F., Tabert, J., Powledge, P., Borriello, G., Schilit, B.N.: Place lab: device positioning using radio beacons in the wild. In: Gellersen, H.-W., Want, R., Schmidt, A. (eds.) Pervasive. Lecture Notes in Computer Science, vol. 3468, pp. 116–133. Springer, Berlin (2005)
14. Leonhardt, U., Magee, J.: Towards a general location service for mobile environments. In: Third IEEE Workshop on Services in Distributed and Networked Environments, pp. 43–50. IEEE, New York (1996)
15. Leonhardt, U., Magee, J.: Multi-sensor location tracking. In: 4th ACM/IEEE Conference on Mobile Computing and Networks (MobiCom), pp. 203–214. ACM, New York (1998)
16. O'Neill, E., Kostakos, V., Kindberg, T., Fatah gen. Schieck, A., Penn, A., Fraser, D.S., Jones, T.: Instrumenting the city: developing methods for observing and understanding the digital cityscape. In: Dourish, P., Friday, A. (eds.) Ubicomp. Lecture Notes in Computer Science, vol. 4206, pp. 315–332. Springer, Berlin (2006)
17. Prakash, R., Baldoni, R.: Causality and the spatial-temporal ordering in mobile systems. Mob. Netw. Appl. **9**(5), 507–516 (2004)
18. Ranganathan, A., Campbell, R.H.: A middleware for context-aware agents in ubiquitous computing environments. In: Middleware, pp. 143–161 (2003)
19. Shekhar, S., Chawla, S.: Spatial Databases—A Tour. Pearson Education, Prentice Hall, Upper Saddle River (2003)
20. Survey, O.: The ellipsoid and the Transverse Mercator projection. Technical Report Geodetic information paper no. 1, version 2.2, Ordnance Survey (1998)
21. Want, R., Hopper, A., Falcao, V., Gibbons, J.: The active badge location system. ACM Trans. Inf. Syst. **10**(1), 91–102 (1992)

Chapter 8
Time Dependent Data

The world is not a static place—the conditions sensors describe vary over time. In some cases the variation is captured as a change in some state (e.g. light as day becomes night), in other cases the variation describes the reading (e.g. a motion detector) and in yet others the reading is encoded within a varying signal (e.g. sound). In this chapter we shall explore some of the techniques which can be applied to handling these time-varying signals.

8.1 Context in Time

As well as considering sensors where a single reading is meaningless we shall develop our use of time in considering sensor data. In Chap. 5 we introduced the idea of states and events. Here we return to these ideas, and the identification of state change and events. In Chap. 6 we considered techniques for mitigating error, including using a stream of sensor readings to use history to help us understand the present. Here we return to the processing of flows of signals. In both cases this chapter's advance is to view context as part of a pattern of states rather than considering only the present.

8.1.1 State Based Systems

The first sort of variation across time we shall consider are systems which change state. Building on the discussion in Chap. 6, the crux here is to differentiate states in the signal from noise. We shall assume that states can be defined in terms of sensor inputs. At some point noise can prevent the accurate detection of states, either because the magnitude of the noise is greater than the signal range occupied by the state, or because the signal is closer to a state boundary than the magnitude of the noise. In this situation we may require a change in processing to better filter the noise, or a more general definition of states that allows graceful degradation. As we

D. Chalmers, *Sensing and Systems in Pervasive Computing*,
Undergraduate Topics in Computer Science,
DOI 10.1007/978-0-85729-841-6_8, © Springer-Verlag London Limited 2011

have seen the process of removing noise often requires multiple readings be taken over time, but this may slow the detection of changes in state. Similarly, transient states (often relating to moving sensors or noise) can be lost in signal processing that favours stability and noise suppression over responsiveness.

States can be defined at three levels: the human interpretation, the system interpretation and the sensor input. At both ends of this chain there is variation in perception and so in the system interpretation there must be room for handling this noise and variation. For a steady underlying state we seek a signal processing system that insulates the human from responses to noise, but properly represents real changes.

At a sensor input level a threshold for change may be set in order to filter out small changes. This may be defined using a call-back interface, as the Phidgets API does, to turn handling changes into an event processing model. The threshold to be chosen may be fixed, according to expected noise in the system; may be determined by the definition of states (as discussed above); or may be defined according to experienced deviation (taking care not to interpret real change as deviation where change is discrete). In Chap. 5 we started to discuss the trade-offs in defining event based and polling sensing, and the need to define high-level interpretations and responses to context which may have discrete conditions which are being identified. These requirements often make detecting *change* as important as a precise measure of state.

Examining sensor data for real differences, even if only trends, is an interesting problem [7]. We noted in Chap. 6 that rapid changes can be identified by comparing slower averages with more responsive models. Models such as this require a definition of what is *significant*, as do models which detect a certain degree (absolute or percentage) change. Where the response to context is well understood (not always straightforward to manage) and exhibits *seams* (step changes or discontinuities) then using the specification of behaviour is a useful approach for defining significance. Where changes are treated in a continuous fashion then change might be defined in terms of normal error, e.g. "a significant change is an order of magnitude larger than the standard deviation noise"; or change could be defined in terms of the user, e.g. by measuring people's typical ability to differentiate between stimuli over a given time-frame and using this as a model of difference, e.g. a majority of people describing two noise levels differently gives that degree of difference as a significant change. It is clear that a good model of the variations experienced is required in order to characterise these models.

Some systems will define response to context as matching particular ranges of values, in this case we can arrange our signal processing to report changes in well-defined ranges. Care needs to be taken in defining the ranges that instability does not occur. Overlapping ranges may be a useful aid here, avoiding changes in state caused by noise at boundaries; similarly a model of state change which has *hysteresis* (change "up" and change "down" happen at different signal levels) might be useful. It is also the case that if some condition makes a "step-change" some sensors and processing algorithms will report intermediate values. In this case requiring some stability before adapting or seeking confirmation might also be useful tactics to avoid mis-reporting the state at those intermediate values.

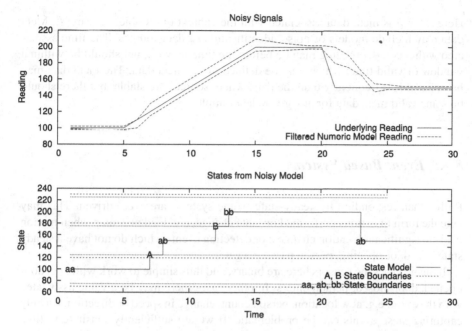

Fig. 8.1 An illustration of a noisy numeric model converting into a hierarchical state model

It is also easy to construct systems which respond to some input in a continuous scale, rather than using discrete conditions. If the changes are sufficiently subtle it may be possible to use raw data; alternatively some simple averaging model might smooth behaviour enough. As discussed in Chap. 6 a model of noise (e.g. mean deviation) might be maintained, and used to filter reported changes further.

In Fig. 8.1 we illustrate an underlying signal being represented by a filter which gives an upper and lower likely bound. This bound is then used to identify which state is to be used. "A" and "B" are more general states which both overlap "ab"; "aa", "ab" and "bb" are narrower state definitions, which should reflect greater certainty about the real conditions. Note that the more general state "A" is used at time 7 where patterns of noise cause the numeric model to fit into neither "aa" nor "ab" during the period of gradual change (and similar later with "B"). In each case the state should be considered to be maintained until a new state is entered, backed up by samples at each unit of the time axis. This model of phenomenon being sampled is considered further in [4]. Higher level state models may be further improved by modelling possible (from external knowledge) or likely (from past use) transitions between states [6]. Such a model may help to avoid incorrect transient values where the underlying model is adjusting to change or suffering from sensor error.

In our notation of context aspects from Chap. 5 we should extend the overall context for an object $\mathbf{C}_o = \bigcup_{\forall a} \mathscr{C}_{a,o}$ to include time (t) and other meta data ($\mathscr{M}$):

$$\mathbf{C}_{o,t} = \bigcup_{\forall a} (\mathscr{C}_{a,o,t'}, \mathscr{M}_{o,t'}) \quad \text{where } (t - t_{window}) \le t' \le t \tag{8.1}$$

Here $\mathcal{M}_{a,o,t'}$ is meta data associated with the context of an object at time t'. Meta data may include models of noise, identification of data sources. The time associated with a context reading may be before the time now (t), but should be within a window of valid time, which may be defined in the meta data. The meta data may be updated less frequently than the data, where sources are stable, but there should be some valid meta data for any given data sample.

8.1.2 Event Based Systems

Rather than responding to steady-states some systems are event driven. This may take the form of actions performed on state change, e.g. load new map when motion leads to significant location changes; or detecting events which do not have a steady state, e.g. door opening, person passing a gate.

In many cases the sensors here are binary, and thus simple to work with, e.g. door opened, door closed, person enters. In other cases there may be a value associated with the event, e.g. new location, person count, change in speed or direction. Cleanly capturing these events can be problematic. If we are sufficiently sensitive to time then we may see states (multiple readings at a level) in these systems, but sampling too infrequently risks missing useful data. The behaviour and deployment of sensors can also cause problems. Various techniques may be deployed here, depending on the situation:

- Use a threshold to determine if an event is significant, balanced against the risk of missing weakly reported events. In this case the system is detecting a transient state, as described above.
- Use a timeout or hysteresis to clean an event which triggers the sensor multiple times, balanced against the risk of missing close events. The is analogous to a "de-bounce filter" in a switch circuit.
- Use a derivative or integral to extract a measure of the event's strength, at the expense of reaction speed. The choice of derivative or integral will depend on the characteristics of the sensor and the meaning of the signal to be extracted.

Having ensured that event models have appropriate filtering they can then be considered in similar ways to context state for many purposes, although their programming is naturally driven by distribution of events rather than querying and monitoring.

8.2 Frequency Domain Models

A rather different sort of time dependent sensor data is that where the variation over time defines the signal, for instance in audio or vibration sensing. Here there is no steady state reading at the physical level.

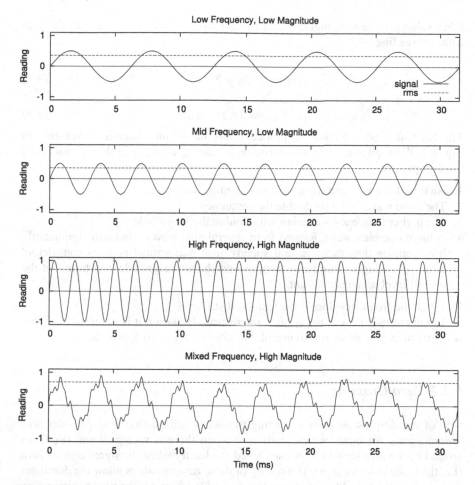

Fig. 8.2 Simple example waveforms and their magnitude

8.2.1 Magnitude

An input, which reads zero when there is no signal and oscillates around zero with a signal will give an average reading of zero (or close to zero) over a sufficient period (a multiple of the lowest frequency component's period). A raw value (or short period of samples) sampled at some random point in time from such an input cannot tell you anything very useful about the magnitude of the signal (beyond a lower bound). In describing the magnitude of oscillating signals it is usual to use one or both of a root-mean-square (RMS) average and an unsigned peak. In both cases these values are usually reported over a period several times longer than the lowest interesting frequency component, so that phase effects are minimised; and are based on samples taken several times more often than the period of the highest interesting frequency component (for the usual reasons of information loss in sampling). An

RMS value gives a meaningful average magnitude, as the square removes the sign from the reading.

$$rms = \sqrt{1/n * \sum_{t=0}^{n} x_t^2} \tag{8.2}$$

$$peak = max(x_t)\forall_{t=0..n}x_t \tag{8.3}$$

The RMS and peak values are plotted for some simple example waveforms in Fig. 8.2. We shall use these waveforms as a running example in this section, note the four phases:

1. An initial wave, a sine wave with a peak magnitude of 1
2. The same wave, but with double the frequency
3. The higher frequency wave, but with double the magnitude
4. A more complex wave, formed from several sine waves—but still significantly less complex than many natural sounds once background noise is considered. Some of the higher frequency components change magnitude over time, but the overall level remains constant.

Note that the frequency does not affect the RMS level.

The magnitude of a signal is often interesting. However, it is often the case that some frequency analysis is also useful. We now explore two approaches to this.

8.2.2 Zero Crossing

One of the simplest ways of extracting frequency information is to consider *zero crossing* rate. An input, which reads zero when there is no signal and oscillates around zero with a signal can be monitored to identify when the signal crosses zero (i.e. the value changes sign). The timing of these zero crossings allow the dominant frequency in the signal to be extracted as $f = 1/2t$ where t is the time between zero crossings and f is the frequency.

Harmonics and high frequency noise can cause the signal to cross zero multiple times around a lower frequencies' zero crossing, so practical systems may have to exclude crossing reports where the signal has not reached some threshold (e.g. some proportion of the recent magnitude). This effect is seen in the more complex wave in Fig. 8.2, where harmonics cause the signal to cross the $y = 0$ axis more than twice for each cycle of the dominant frequency in the signal. Such a model simply indicates the dominant frequency, but is computationally simple and suffices for many applications, e.g. [3].

8.2.3 Fourier Transforms

We do not present the Fourier transform in a full mathematical way here: a good engineering maths textbook will do that and set it in the proper context of complex numbers, integration etc. The key formulae are shown, to remind the familiar. For other readers not inclined to learn the mathematical techniques, it is still useful to be aware of this means for transforming data from one dimension into another. The most important application in the context of this course is in turning a time— magnitude varying signal (plotted on a graph of time against level as in Fig. 8.2) into a frequency—magnitude domain signal (plotted on a graph of frequency against level). Audio and vibration data are the obvious examples, but the technique is applicable to the radio spectrum and to very slowly varying signals as well. The principle is also applicable to other multi-dimensional data.

In outline, the principle of the transform is that a complex waveform can be built by combining sine and cosine waves at various frequencies and magnitudes. For example, the final waveform in Fig. 8.2 is built from just five constituent sine waves. The transform leads from a function $f(x)$ giving magnitude at time x to the Fourier transform parametrised by frequency $\hat{f}(\omega)$:

$$\hat{f}(\omega) = \frac{1}{\sqrt{2\pi}} \int_{-\infty}^{\infty} f(x) \cdot e^{-i\omega x} \, dx \tag{8.4}$$

For practical purposes the continuous and rather large range of times in the Fourier transform needs to be simplified. The discrete Fourier transform (DFT) is used to achieve this. A finite series of samples is used, which can analyse the input from a distinct period in time with an upper frequency limit determined by the sample frequency. The equation is transformed from an integral over infinite time to a sum of a finite series, giving the DFT of a frequency F_n:

$$F_n = \frac{1}{\sqrt{2\pi}} \sum_{k=0}^{N-1} f_k \cdot e^{ikn/N} \tag{8.5}$$

Where f_k is the sample of magnitude at time t_k, over N samples. The time interval represented by each step in k should be constant. Comparing the output of a Fourier transform with a DFT will be like comparing a continuous function with a histogram: the shape will be similar, but with discrete groupings of the data.

· Example DFTs for the waveforms in Fig. 8.2 are plotted in Fig. 8.3. In the top plot we see the three simple examples together, each impulse representing a single sine wave of a given frequency and magnitude. In the lower plot we see the five components of the signal plotted together. Natural harmonics (powers of 2) were chosen for the frequencies, except the lower one, and these are illustrated by the equally spaced impulses on the log-scale x axis. Three DFTs have been performed, representing the start, middle and end of the time of the input. The x axis for the later two has been shifted slightly for clarity on the page. As two of the components have varying magnitude this is seen in the changes in height of those frequency components. Note that there are no frequency components of these signals between the sine waves which compose them. A DFT which included noise, multiple sources, or non-sine waves, e.g. square, saw-tooth, would have a rather more complex set of impulses across the spectrum.

The DFT will generally have a complexity $O(N^2)$. For our applications a fast Fourier transform (FFT) [1] is often used as it greatly simplifies the algorithms to

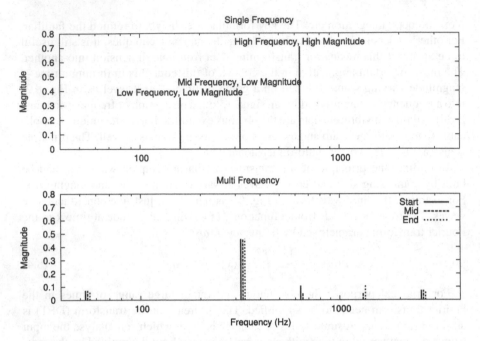

Fig. 8.3 Example discrete Fourier transform outputs for example time series data

be used at the expense of a reasonable restriction in the number of samples used, reducing complexity to $O(N \log N)$, without requiring more data store. The FFT is a family of algorithms which compute DFTs. There are variants, but the core principle of many is to divide the DFT into multiple DFTs with smaller size N (typically $N/2$). This allows common multipliers to be factored out, simplifying the equation and repeated division results in many simple calculations which can be re-combined, taking advantage of previously calculated values. Although simpler, expectations of detail and frequency range need to be raised with care when more CPU and memory limited devices are being considered—a DSP or specialised ALU functions are often deployed for best performance, as the FFT involves large numbers of multiply-add computations. The division of the input values in half also constrains the samples to be of some power of two in size in the simpler versions of the algorithm, although the general case allows other divisions of the data. The process becomes:

1. Divide the input data $x = x_0, \dots, x_{N-1}$ into even (E) and odd (O) indexed values with M values in each:

$$E = x_{2m} \quad \text{and} \quad O = x_{2m+1} \quad \text{where } m = 0, \dots, N/2 - 1 \quad (8.6)$$

2. Re-divide until the base case of a single complex value x_0 is reached for E and O.
3. Call the FFT computation for each of these divided values and then combine, as follows:
   a. The base case single values *odd* and *even* are simply returned, otherwise these arrays are obtained from the previous step

  b. Step through the data, $k = 0, \ldots, M$
  c. Compute $f_k = e^{-2\pi i k / M}$
  d. Compute the low-index value and high index values:

$$Y_k = even_k + f_k \cdot odd_k \tag{8.7}$$

$$Y_{k+M/2} = even_k - f_k \cdot odd_k \tag{8.8}$$

4. Return the final Y of size N.

Having processed the data to obtain the frequency components these can be used to model the world. Common techniques are to look for the presence (beyond noise) of certain frequencies, or the relative levels of certain frequencies to identify conditions, e.g. presence of a signal source with that signal pattern.

8.3 Prediction

Obviously prediction of future values and removing error from past values can be useful to undertake, if those predictions can be reliable. The benefits are clear from the discussion of effort required in polling in Sect. 5.5: by predicting the future we can take less frequent readings, perform less processing of data and, probably most importantly, we can avoid communicating new readings so frequently.

It is often the case that prediction over limited time can be undertaken from good models of the recent situation. Removing noise from historical readings can apply similar techniques to those described as well, with the added advantage of being able to use what happened after the time of interest (as well as before) to inform the model of that time. Longer term prediction can also be undertaken, by gathering sufficient additional information—often in the form of historical patterns.

8.3.1 Recent Trends

Simply put, the basic approach to prediction is to look at the recent past and extrapolate. But, as the banks say "values can go down as well as up", growth never continues for ever, so this is a limited tool! A second order prediction will fit curves rather than straight lines to the past data and will consider saturation values. From examination of the past a limited prediction will be made, looking forward only as far as the data suggests the prediction might hold for.

In considering the scope of prediction we should consider two factors: whether we continue sensing and can revoke a prediction once it becomes invalid; and what degree of error we can bear. Although continuing sensing requires ongoing power to the sensor and CPU, if the predicted reading avoids repeated network use it may have significant benefit. The second factor gives rise to consideration of how good the prediction is. A projection which is slightly wrong in its gradient or curve will gradually become less and less accurate. We must know how large a deviation is acceptable before we need to issue a new reading. This gives rise to considerations about how data is interpreted and applied in context awareness again. A model of data which accepts variation, such as ranges or distributions, may be of benefit here.

It is possible to incorporate derivative models into a Kalman or Particle filter, for instance using speed derived from a sequence of locations influence the model of expected location. These models can aid with prediction of low-level values and also with higher level models of context [6].

8.3.2 Interpolation and Related Sensors

As well as using the past to predict properties we can use knowledge of other nearby sensors. By forming a map with sensor contours we can interpolate readings between the lines. By storing a spatio-temporal history (or by defined knowledge) we can find out which sensors are closely related and infer local readings which are expected to be similar [2].

It is possible to incorporate additional sensors into a Particle filter, for instance using accelerometers to affect the prediction of location. Where acceleration changes, e.g. turning a corner, recent trends in location cease to be applicable; where acceleration is variable in one direction, e.g. a straight road with junctions, then recent speed is not a linear predictor of future location but the direction of movement is still useful.

8.3.3 Long-Term History

Significantly better predictions about repeated patterns of sensing are possible if data store to hold longer histories is available. Even without knowing about the Earth spinning many predictions can be made about likely changes in sensor readings caused by sunrise if a few days data are collected. Similarly, longer histories can be used to better constrain the simplistic extrapolations from recent history we considered above.

The downside of long term histories is that patterns can take a lot of data and CPU power to detect, and handling of changes in the underlying patterns can be hard. Detecting weekends, public holidays, vacations, seasons, school terms, moving house or office, changing car etc are all both hard and significant. A model which relies on patterns is inclined to break when the pattern changes: either while a new pattern is formed, e.g. moving house, school terms, or in how feedback to the existing pattern is handled (e.g. seasons).

8.3.4 Learning

In Sect. 5.5 we described rules which define response to context. We returned to specifying behaviour in Sect. 6.4, however it is clear that rules could be written so that the most likely context triggers the behaviour, or to specify reactions as being valid for a range of contexts. An alternative approach uses experience to develop the response to context: learning. When a new (or at least one where the response is unclear, default staring positions might be programmed in) situation occurs the user is asked what the correct response is. When an inappropriate response is given, the user corrects the behaviour and the correction is learnt. Over time this teaching process gives rise to a model of context. As new context conditions occur the system must try to identify (or ask) what it is that differentiates this context from others already identified. As sensors change the new data at lower context stack levels needs to be translated into the higher level model—the experienced and learnt context probably remains valid.

This approach has disadvantages:

- It interrupts the user or requires significant training data.
- It may not lead to a model which is easy to understand and reuse, e.g. for new applications or new users.
- When the learning is being corrected identifying the scope of new contexts is not trivial and it is hard to separate evolving use of the application (e.g. finding quicker ways of working which require a different response not a different model of context) from evolving contexts experienced by the user (e.g. changes to task for a new job make the old context and associated responses redundant) from evolving models of context (i.e. genuinely refining a model due to new situations).

8.4 Summary

In this chapter we have considered three issues around the theme of time:

1. How context can be placed in time. Considering the annotation of context values with time of reading so that a sequence of context emerges, rather than just the conditions "now". The processing of context into states, and the resulting sequences of state with underlying readings was shown. This then naturally leads to a series of events—either for momentary conditions or indicating state change.
2. Sensor values not only show different states through time, but may encode their state in the variation over time. We examined common techniques, in particular the fast Fourier transform to analyse such data.
3. Finally, we considered prediction and some techniques that can be brought to bear here.

In each case the understanding of previous chapters on context and error are relevant to the extension to consider time, and location continues to be a useful example of context which varies over time.

8.5 Suggested Readings

- An introduction to the treatment of time (and space) in context data: Philip D. Gray and Daniel Salber. Modelling and using sensed context information in the design of interactive applications. In Murray Reed Little and Laurence Nigay, editors, *EHCI*, volume 2254 of *Lecture Notes in Computer Science*, pages 317–336. Springer, 2001
- An examination of balancing change detection with noise resistant averages: M. Kim and B.D. Noble. Mobile network estimation. In *7th ACM Conference on Mobile Computing and Networking (MobiCom)*, Rome, Italy, 2001
- An study of context inference using frequency and magnitude models of audio input from water pipes: James Fogarty, Carolyn Au, and Scott E. Hudson. Sensing from the basement: a feasibility study of unobtrusive and low-cost home activity recognition. In Pierre Wellner and Ken Hinckley, editors, *UIST*, pages 91–100. ACM, 2006
- The use of Bayesian filters in forming high level, predictive, models of context from low level data: Donald Patterson, Lin Liao, Dieter Fox, and Henry Kautz. Inferring high-level behavior from low-level sensors. In *UbiComp 2003: Ubiquitous Computing*, pages 73–89. Springer, 2003

8.6 Laboratory Exercises: Motion Sensors

This lab builds on the ideas of context, but introduces us to signals where variation is of interest. Motion sensors (IR or ultrasonic) are ideal, and other sensors (magnetic, vibration, accelerometers, light (and shadow)) can be arranged to give similar signal patterns. In detecting motion we are interested in signals which are changing—a moving object to sense will rarely give a "state" type reading. This means that averaging based approaches to noise reduction from Chap. 6 are no longer useful on the raw sensor data.

In order to construct a visible response LEDs might be used, either as a movement alarm; to simulate a room light which switches off when no-one is in; or to indicate direction of movement. Text output and GUIs are equally valid output mechanisms.

Consider using some mix of change detection by value and by differential and filter and pattern matching techniques—build on prior experience in other courses where appropriate. If there are several lab groups it might be useful to arrange for each to take a different approach and to compare results at the end. This lab could lead into the next.

8.7 Laboratory Exercises: People Detection in a Large Space

The purpose of this lab is to build on previous experience with the behaviour of Phidgets sensors and the way in which sensors can tell you more than might be expected.

This experiment works best in a large space, where the arrangement of the room and lighting are controllable. However, the principles could be adapted to any space, although having good control over the environment makes things simpler.

The Problem Play a game, which might be thought of as a "burglar alarm" or a variation on "grandmother's footsteps". The goal is to detect an approaching person from as far away as possible.

Sensors designed to detect motion of humans would be the obvious choice here, but this seems like less of a challenge than being able to interpret other aspects of the environment, which might be presented as context, and use them to detect presence. This is a vital part of sensor processing, as presence which can affect sensors clearly needs to be understood when applying sensor data. Detecting presence might be extended in real systems to detecting aspects of context for which there is no "sensor": task, activity etc. In this spirit, it is suggested that light sensors are the first to be distributed (having control over room lighting helps here). Others, such as vibration sensors and microphones, and then motion sensors, could be added to vary the challenge.

1. Understand the space you are working in: what environmental factors can you control; how big is it etc.
2. Understand the sensors you are using—it is hoped that the previous labs will have given you a good idea of necessary sampling rates, signals produced by different sensors, likely variations for signal vs. noise, etc.
3. If the space, task and groups are introduced in advance a little planning before the session is strongly advised.
4. Organise a computer at one end of your space. Arrange your environment and sensors and processing in various ways to arrive at a detection system. Long leads and working in pairs or threes are advised here.

The Test Members of other teams move through each others spaces and detections (real with distance or false) are recorded. In the first instance the detecting party has control over the environment. If this proves too simple then the party being detected might be allowed some changes to the environment. To turn the exercise into a competition, teams gain points by detecting from far away (count in floor tiles) and loose points for false positives.

8.8 Laboratory Exercises: Accelerometers

This lab uses 2 or 3 axis accelerometers. These can provide various sorts of data, requiring different processing:

1. Per-axis acceleration either as continuous data, short term averages, detecting changes or integrated to describe larger scale movement. Compare some of these reporting approaches with different inputs (e.g. gesture, orientation, gait) and consider their effectiveness (speed of response and accuracy).

2. Capture gross acceleration across axes, by combining as sides of a triangle ($a = \sqrt{x^2 + y^2 + z^2}$).
3. Capture level of vibration, by separating small-time-scale variation from larger movements. This may build most easily onto gross acceleration. It may also be possible to extract frequency of vibration information with a suitable sampling rate and period.

The use of accelerometers can be compared to other means of detecting movement, such as motion sensors, range finders, and vibration sensors from the analogue Phidgets.

8.9 Laboratory Exercises: Sound

Connect a microphone to a computer, sample the input into an array once per second (a fairly simple process with Java) and perform magnitude and frequency analysis. Use this to build a model of context, appropriate to your situation. For instance:

- Differentiate background noise from talking and/or music.
- Identify loud events, such as a door being knocked or closing or someone clapping.
- Differentiate between speakers in a conversation. To what extent is the difference due to position relative to the microphone and due to different voices.
- Recognise environmental noises: taps running, kettle boiling, car starting etc.

References

1. Cooley, J.W., Tukey, J.W.: An algorithm for the machine calculation of complex Fourier series. Math. Comput. **19**, 297–301 (1965)
2. Deshpande, A., Guestrin, C., Madden, S.: Using probabilistic models for data management in acquisitional environments. In: CIDR, pp. 317–328 (2005)
3. Fogarty, J., Au, C., Hudson, S.E.: Sensing from the basement: a feasibility study of unobtrusive and low-cost home activity recognition. In: Wellner, P., Hinckley, K. (eds.) UIST, pp. 91–100. ACM, New York (2006)
4. Gray, P.D., Salber, D.: Modelling and using sensed context information in the design of interactive applications. In: Little, M.R., Nigay, L. (eds.) EHCI. Lecture Notes in Computer Science, vol. 2254, pp. 317–336. Springer, Berlin (2001)
5. Kim, M., Noble, B.D.: Mobile network estimation. In: 7th ACM Conference on Mobile Computing and Networking (MobiCom), Rome, Italy, 2001
6. Patterson, D., Liao, L., Fox, D., Kautz, H.: Inferring high-level behavior from low-level sensors. In: UbiComp 2003: Ubiquitous Computing, pp. 73–89. Springer, Berlin (2003)
7. Tolle, G., Polastre, J., Szewczyk, R., Culler, D.E., Turner, N., Tu, K., Burgess, S., Dawson, T., Buonadonna, P., Gay, D., Hong, W.: A macroscope in the redwoods. In: Redi, J., Balakrishnan, H., Zhao, F. (eds.) SenSys, pp. 51–63. ACM, New York (2005)

Chapter 9
Sensor Networking

9.1 Introduction: Purpose of- and Issues in- Sensor Networks

Sensor networks are a research area that has grown from ad-hoc, mobile networking and shares some concerns with pervasive computing. A good introduction to the issues can be found in Estrin et al.'s 1999 paper [3], where the following challenges were identified:

- To provide for information gathering by unattended devices, possibly in inhospitable terrain. The focus of the devices is on sensing, with computation and networking in place to facilitate this goal. The lifetime of the sensors (between maintenance visits) must be great, which again implies low power consumption.
- Through using cheap devices the numbers of deployed sensors can be greater than in the past and over a wider area. This scale leads to more useful data but also challenges in designing effective algorithms (a single broadcast network is not feasible) and a further requirement for minimal maintenance and adaptation to failure.
- The applicability to many domains, both physical and in the dynamics and use of data, requires not custom designs but a general purpose approach to their design.
- To achieve these goals sensors should be able to self-organise, to coordinate local (node and area) efforts to maximise their lifetime and the effectiveness of the collected data.

The example of deployment in the paper is "several thousand sensors are . . . thrown from an aircraft in remote terrain"—which is a good indication of the requirement for large-scale, wide area self-organisation. The exemplar in Chap. 1 of habitat monitoring [18] raises similar issues. The weaknesses of existing routing approaches to meet resource constraints are illustrated in [5].

Networks in the internet sense are a set of autonomous nodes sharing a common infrastructure to achieve their own goals by forming connections as needed with any other node in the network. Sensor networks have a rather different purpose: to collect and transport data from many sources to a small number of sinks, in order to achieve a task. The network is a collaborative effort working to achieve a number

D. Chalmers, *Sensing and Systems in Pervasive Computing*,
Undergraduate Topics in Computer Science,
DOI 10.1007/978-0-85729-841-6_9, © Springer-Verlag London Limited 2011

of tasks defined by a small proportion of the nodes (the sinks)—in many cases a single task defined at deployment time. However, the sensor network nodes are also different to traditional networked computers: they are unattended, simpler and more numerous. This different top level approach gives rise to various differences in the design of sensor network systems: Connections form according to need, particularly where sensors are mobile. Data rather than devices are the most significant entity. Collaboration to achieve the effective transport of data while maximising lifetime require different routing techniques to the Internet.

Sensor networks are slightly apart from the treatment of pervasive computing so far, which has focused on context awareness for the user. The fields are different, but the techniques and considerations of sensor networks overlap with pervasive computing. Sensor networks may enable some of context awareness, and the approach to ad-hoc organisation and power sensitivity are important to learn from.

9.2 Ad-Hoc Network Routing

Before tackling sensor networks, per se, we shall take a brief look at ad-hoc networks. Often sensor networks look like ad-hoc networks, and ad-hoc networks reflect the needs of pervasive computing in general, so we shall open with a comparison of ad-hoc, sensor and internet connectivity:

- **Infrastructure** Ad-hoc networks are defined by a lack of fixed, managed infrastructure. Sensor networks often have this characteristic to some extent, but also often have specialised last-hops to connect to remote data sinks. The internet has an extensive infrastructure.
- **Routing Structure** In comparison to Internet networking ad-hoc and sensor networks lack the managed organisation-driven hierarchy of identities and devices. For instance the role of router is more likely to be defined by hardware in the internet and by position in an ad-hoc network. This also leads to a need for flexible roles and responsive configuration.
- **Communication patterns** Sensor networks tend to have patterns of communication of many sources to a few sinks, which can simplify some protocols while internet and general ad-hoc protocols have less well defined roles.
- **Mobility** None of these networks is defined by mobility. The internet has developed to use wireless links, mobile IP etc. to support mobility. Ad-hoc networks, due to the lack of infrastructure, make mobility a reasonable assumption. Sensor networks often rely on long-running queries, which makes mobility more of a challenge than in ad-hoc networks—and location more likely to be a feature of the data being sensed where it does occur.
- **Per Hop Behaviour** Ad-hoc and sensor networks typically use wireless networks, so the scope of a hop is less well defined and multicast is cheap, compared to the point-to-point hop behaviour typified in the internet.
- **Distant Data** Ad-hoc and sensor networks generally have limitations (e.g. bandwidth, power, reliability, lack of two-way communication) that make dynamic

retrieval of distant managed information, as in DNS, and use of centralised services undesirable.

9.2.1 Ad-Hoc On-Demand Distance Vector Routing

The Ad-hoc On-Demand Distance Vector Routing protocol (AODV) [15] is a classic ad-hoc networking protocol, responding to the needs of that scenario without placing specific requirements on the underlying link protocols. We shall describe this here, not as the best protocol for some situation, but as an example of the approaches and issues which you will find elsewhere if you research this topic further. The material in this section is based on the description in [15].

AODV targets small computers, rather than sensor devices, but makes the assumption that they are freely mobile. This implies that the current set of neighbours routinely changes. The protocol is "on-demand" in the sense of participation: nodes only participate in the protocol when they lie on an active path; neither do nodes maintain routing data for nodes which they are not communicating with (either as end points or as routers). This on-demand nature is a good match for the mobile scenario, as routes may come into- and go out of existence without being used. When awareness of other nodes is needed local broadcasts are used to identify neighbours—but a primary objective is to use discovery broadcasts only when necessary.

The discovery protocol makes use of two counters: a monotonically increasing sequence number (`src_seq_num`) and a `broadcast_id`. The protocol operates as follows:

1. When a source needs to communicate with a node and has no routing information for it a route request packet is broadcast to its neighbours. This contains: `src_addr, src_seq_num, broadcast_id, dest_addr, dest_seq _num, hop_count`. The `src_addr` and `broadcast_id` uniquely identify a request as the `broadcast_id` is incremented for each request.
2. Each neighbour either sends a reply to the source (see next), if it can provide a route; or increments the `hop_count` and broadcasts to its neighbours. A cache of request identifiers is kept, so that each request is only acted on once—as wireless nodes may well have overlapping reception ranges or loops may be created in the broadcasts. Nodes which forward the request also keeps note of the `src_addr, src_seq_num, broadcast_id` and `dest_addr` in order to have a reverse path in its routing table ready for any response, or other requests for communication with the source node. This entry also has an expiry time. The routing table `src_seq_num` is maintained with each packet seen from that node. The `dest_seq_num` specifies the required freshness of the route—by specifying the minimum value the sequence number entry for that destination can have in the routing table for a response by that node to be allowed.
3. A reply to the request, either from an intermediate node or the destination itself, will contain: `source_addr, dest_addr, dest_seq_num, hop_count,`

`lifetime`. The nodes on the path will have seen the request (assuming symmetric paths are possible) and so have a route to the original source; as they process the route reply they update their routing tables to reflect the newly discovered path to the original destination. No entry was made while processing the request as the forwarding was speculative and a large proportion of nodes would not expect to see a response. Duplicate replies are forwarded if they are fresher (by sequence number) or have a smaller hop count, otherwise they are discarded.

4. As nodes move and become unreachable the process may be re-run. The break can be identified by the node immediately upstream; and source nodes should check that they expect to need to send new packets before re-running the protocol. In many practical scenarios the movement will be incremental and a new route can be found near to the break.

Due to the use of flooding the performance of this protocol varies with the network size: the number of nodes increases the number of messages involved in the discovery process and also (in a scenario with uniform node behaviour) the number of discoveries in a time period. However, the use of these broadcasts is minimised, loop-free routes are produced and response to link failure is quick. Simulations in the original paper showed that despite the flooding these approaches led to useful latency and scalability in area and number of nodes.

9.2.2 Clusters

As for any large network, global knowledge of identities, paths or structure is not a practical proposal. The source routing approach in Dynamic Source Routing (DSR) [9] does not provide global knowledge, but does require nodes to maintain a map of intermediate routes and perform whole-path routing decisions. Both these issues are expensive when considering the applicability of ad-hoc network protocols to the sensor network scenario.

Where data tends to flow in or out of "hot-spots" nodes near these points will tend to see more packets and so consume energy faster. For instance, in Fig. 9.1 nodes A, B, C and D are all neighbours to the sink. However, node C is routing data from three other nodes, which means that it may be communicating seven times as much data as one of the edge nodes (assuming the communication is driven by regular samples and data are not combined). Where their power supply is a battery this causes a problem of network longevity—not because a large number of nodes have no power, but because a few critical nodes have no power. Where hot-spots are stable one solution is to provide these nodes with improved power supplies. Where the network can form into clusters this tends to concentrate traffic through a few nodes, which may help in choosing such extra deployment. This approach is most effective with controllable radio power output, so the cluster heads can give longer network hops. This has two effects: first it reduces the number of transmissions required of any given packet. It also reduces the traffic flowing through nodes near the cause of the hot spot by transmitting across them (typically where the hot-spot

Fig. 9.1 An example sensor
network, with nodes near the
sink (white) more heavily
loaded than nodes at the edge

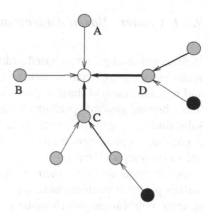

is around a sink). This "smears" the hot-spot, spreading the load over more nodes
while loading each less heavily. If the cluster heads can be renegotiated then as
their power is depleted they can return to the role of ordinary node. Now a simpler
alternative model for deployment in stable hot-spots is also possible: to provide
additional nodes (possibly without sensors) to form part of the sacrificial routing
cluster and so balance the lifetime at the cluster level in order to maintain network
lifetime [6].

9.3 Data Driven Networks

Rather than have sinks periodically polling sensors by name, sensor networks generally allow the data to drive the communications. A *query* is sent into the network
and the nodes use this to decide what data is interesting. In the general case sensor
networks are ad-hoc and may include mobile nodes, so that global identifiers and
node based routing are hard to work with—but the data centric approach means that
global device identifiers are not needed. Instead queries define interest in data and
the data is sent where it is found to be interesting. Another benefit of this model
is that it can be used to combine data from multiple sensors, so saving energy and
spatial-bandwidth use by reducing the number of packets to be sent.

In order to meet the scale challenges of sensor networks algorithms which define local (to each sensor) interactions working towards a common goal without
central coordination are required. *Directed diffusion* [3, 8] is one model for this behaviour. In this model node identities need only be local, for instance to remove
loops and agree on any clustering, while addresses and routing are expressed using
the data. This locality has the attractive property that algorithms that reflect it scale
much better than algorithms with central coordination and are more robust in the
face of individual node failure or network partition. We shall introduce the model
through content based addressing first, which is not particular to sensor networks,
and then consider a few of the many approaches found in sensor networking. Finally
in Sect. 9.6 we introduce the idea of location into this data centric model.

9.3.1 Content Based Addressing

Before considering content based addressing in sensor networks, we shall review its wider use. A more detailed survey [1] might be useful reading for the unfamiliar and forms the basis of the discussion here. Content based addressing is used in publish/subscribe systems (pub/sub) to facilitate the routing of data from publishers to subscribers, using the data rather than lists of identifiers as the basis for routing. The decoupling of publishers from subscribers has properties which are often desirable, such as privacy and scalability.

A subscriber describes their interests as constraints in a type system which describes potential content (more on this later). A publisher provides meta-data describing publications which place it in this type system. The infrastructure then compares the meta-data with the subscriptions it holds and forwards the data to subscribers where each attribute of the data meets the constraints. To function this requires a routing system, with an infrastructure for storing subscriptions and matching data to them, and then forwarding the subscriptions and/or data through the network (often over an overlay peer-to-peer network) to facilitate distribution.

The description system gives rise to several variations on the pub/sub theme, including:

- A set of *topics* are defined, which define channels between publishers who generate data on that topic and subscribers who are interested. The type system is quite coarse grained, with subscriptions simply being a list of topics. The advantage is that routing can be quite simple, but at the expense of expression—although hierarchy can be used in topic definition.
- Conditions may be described over the *content* of data, removing the separation between data and meta-data and describing subscriptions in terms of the data. This approach is more expressive than topics, but also more complex and leads to more dynamic correspondence between publishers and subscribers.
- Some simplification of content-based pub/sub can be had by using ontologies to model the *concepts* being communicated. This approach makes the description of content more systematic, but retains the dynamic nature and some scope for expressive subscriptions.
- The *type* of the data, in the general programming sense, may be used to describe subscriptions. This model is applicable when a type system provides sufficient differentiation between data to be useful.
- Finally, *location* is sometimes used to describe the data from mobile publishers, or publishers with geo-tagged data, e.g. [4]. Subscriptions in this case will describe matches between space, as described in Chap. 7.

The infrastructure may be organised in a number of ways, most commonly:

- A network of *brokers*, which form a managed overlay.
- A *structured peer-to-peer* overlay, where node status and relationships are unmanaged. The peer-to-peer algorithm is designed to maintain coverage of the subscription space and handle a more dynamic membership than the broker scheme.

Over this infrastructure routing may be achieved by flooding publications, flooding subscriptions, a selective mechanism such as rendezvous and filters, or gossiping. Gossiping gives a probabilistic algorithm, with unstructured routes, which find paths in highly dynamic networks, such as MANETs; the other approaches are deterministic. Each approach has a different position with respect to overheads, limitations in subscription expression, handling dynamic nodes and handling dynamic subscriptions:

- Publication flooding has no overhead in storing subscriptions and no limitations in what those subscriptions can express, but does not scale with increasing network size unless a large proportion of nodes are interested in a large proportion of publications.
- Subscription flooding provides each node complete knowledge of all subscribers, which does not scale with frequent subscription changes. In pervasive computing it is easy to imagine context based subscriptions being quite dynamic and so not suitable for this approach. However, no publications are unnecessarily forwarded and on joining a node can easily find a place in the routing.
- Selective rendezvous makes use of two functions, which map a publication to a node list and a subscription to a node list, through a transformation from the attributes of the content based addressing to the identity space of nodes. A node receiving a publication checks whether it is one of the nodes returned by the function and if so sends the data to matching subscriptions; otherwise it forwards the data to all the nodes listed. A node receiving a subscription checks whether it is in the list of nodes returned for that subscription, if so it adds the subscription to its list, otherwise it forwards the subscription. This check and forward approach can work with peer-to-peer networks which require multiple hops to reach an address. Eventually data will be meet subscriptions at *rendezvous* nodes. The definition of the transformation functions is not trivial and tends to limit the expression in the subscription language. Adding or removing nodes to the system is expensive, but the approach reduces the duplication of effort and can be scalable in delivery of data.
- Selective filters forward only those publications which match the subscriptions' constraints for a given link. Each subscription change may therefore cause a change to propagate through the whole network, as for flooding. However, it is not necessary for every subscription to reach every publisher directly, as subscriptions which match or overlap can be combined into a single more general subscription—and published data need only flow down a link once to service many such subscriptions. Over a highly dynamic network, or dynamic overlay, maintaining correct routing tables can cause a considerable overhead.
- Gossip routing involves nodes contacting a few others, typically either at random or neighbours assigned at random or through some name space locality or *local* information about interests, and passing data on—and possibly receiving some back. This gossiping progresses in rounds, allowing the data to spread through the network despite any changes in topology as discovery is typically a part of the partnering process. The protocol is simple and requires no routing tables, complete picture of state, central control, or complex mapping algorithms (although

loop detection may be used). However, delay can be very variable (the protocol is probabilistic after all) and the path of any given data is unlikely to be optimum.

In applying content based routing to mobile, ad-hoc and sensor networks, the structure of the underlying network and the data to be transferred informs choice of algorithms. Location awareness and mobility in the network are discussed in [4]. There may not be a global naming scheme or a well defined route across the network, and overlay networks in the internet peer-to-peer sense are harder to arrange. Constraints on store and processing may impose limits on routing tables, subscription store, etc. Some degree of churn (arrival and departure of nodes) might be anticipated, although less so in many sensor networks. Despite these constraints, the separation of data sources from consumers and description of routing by content rather than identity are attractive in networks where identity may be weak and data flows are often not point-to-point but from a few producers to many consumers.

9.4 An Overview of Sensor Network Routing Protocols

Sensor networks have some similar properties to ad-hoc networks, such as: arbitrary and possibly mobile nodes, wireless connectivity and the need to scale to large numbers of nodes. This suggests existing protocols, such as AODV [15] or DSR [9] might be appropriate. However, both these require flooding for discovery, which is undesirable in sensor networks. Sensor networks are also characterised by limited device capability, e.g. memory size and energy, and data-driven rather than node-driven communications patterns. So, while the lessons of ad-hoc networking should be remembered the problem—and hence the solution—may be different.

An appropriate routing algorithm depends on the characteristics of the network and the application: its topology, e.g. mesh or tree; whether multi-cast comes for free in the radio link; constraints on delay and energy consumption; the stability of the topology; the communications patterns required by query and data transmission etc.

In this section we present a pair of classic protocols: Directed Diffusion and SPIN and then consider the use of location in sensor network routing. Newer protocols, with various improvements and specialisations exist, but understanding this early work gives a good basis for further research. The interested reader might also wish to consider a comparison of protocols, a good example which considers energy, delay and node exhaustion as its basis can be found in [11]—but there are many others.

9.4.1 Sensor Protocols for Information via Negotiation

Sensor Protocols for Information via Negotiation (SPIN) [5] is a family of protocols designed for "dissemination of individual sensor observations to all the sensors in a network, treating all sensors as potential sink nodes". The following discussion is based on that in the original paper. The SPIN protocols offer an advantage over flooding approach of typical ad-hoc network protocols. These problems include:

- Implosion, where multiple paths cause the same information to arrive several times, from a single source.
- Overlap, where overlapping sensor coverage causes the same information to arrive several times, from different sources.
- Resource blindness, where behaviour does not reflect capacity, in particular energy supply.

In order to avoid implosion and overlap the transmission of data is negotiated, using meta-data and the tools of content based networks. Resources are monitored locally and some behaviour, such as routing, adapted accordingly. The protocol must be able to reduce the exchange of data by more than the overhead of the meta data to be beneficial, but in a sensor network application the data flows may be sufficiently complex or long lived for this to be the case. The format of the meta-data is left as an application specific detail, a loss-less underlying network is assumed.

SPIN has three types of message, the first two containing only meta data and so are smaller:

1. Meta data advertisements of new data from a source.
2. Requests to receive the actual data described in an advert.
3. Data messages, containing actual sensor data and a meta data header to allow this to be matched to requests.

These message types also correspond to protocol phases:

1. When a node has new data to share an advert describing this data is sent. On receipt of an advert a node will check whether it already has, or has requested, data with matching meta data. It is assumed that data whose meta data is identical offers no advantage to the system as this represents implosion or overlap.
2. If the meta data is new then a request message requesting data is sent. No reply is given where the data is not required. Not all data need be requested: only that which is new need be specified.
3. When a request is received by the source node the data is sent. The recipient now has new data and so performs phase one of the protocol with its neighbours, other than the source. If the recipient has its own data to send, or data from several sources, it can aggregate this data and advertise this aggregation.

The protocol is illustrated in a small network in Fig. 9.2, including the non-request of already requested data and the advertising on of received data.

Data may be re-advertised from time to time: to recover from loss (with some delay) or when its neighbour list changes, reflecting node mobility. Changes to topology are reflected locally, and distant sources and destinations can remain unaware. Each node performs only local processing, not requiring global information to proceed.

There is an energy aware variant of the protocol, SPIN-2. When resources are plentiful it operates as above. When a node has depleted its energy the protocol is

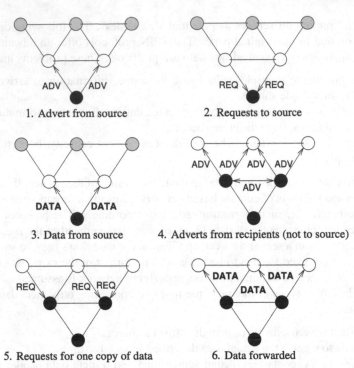

Fig. 9.2 The SPIN-1 protocol illustrated, based on [5], word size/weight indicates message size. Wendi Rabiner Heinzelman, Joanna Kulik, and Hari Balakrishnan. Adaptive protocols for information dissemination in wireless sensor networks. In *Proceedings of the 5th annual ACM/IEEE international conference on Mobile computing and networking*, MobiCom '99, pages 174–185, New York, NY, USA, 1999. ACM, http://doi.acm.org/10.1145/313451.313529. © 1999 Association for Computing Machinery, Inc. Reprinted by permission

modified, on the basis that it will not engage in a phase of the protocol if it cannot complete the other stages. Further variants on SPIN have been proposed, which take advantage of broadcast networks; offer negotiation of forwarding which considers resource availability; and improve reliability over lossy networks have been proposed.

9.4.2 Directed Diffusion

Directed diffusion [8] was another early sensor network protocol, which illustrates the idea of local processing and content based addressing clearly.

We describe the process below (drawing on the description in [8]) and illustrate it in Fig. 9.3. Network nodes are depicted as having local broadcast indicated by the links in the network graph. The *sink* is the white node near the top and the sources are the black nodes near the bottom.

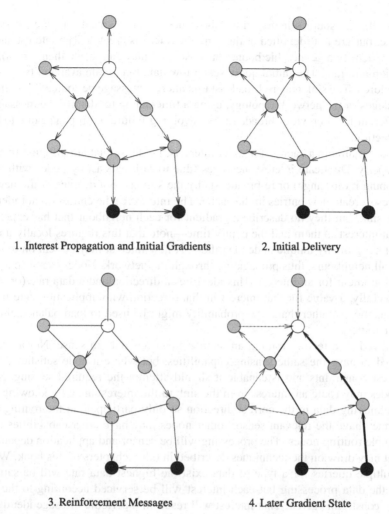

1. Interest Propagation and Initial Gradients   2. Initial Delivery

3. Reinforcement Messages   4. Later Gradient State

Fig. 9.3 Directed diffusion illustrated, based on [8], line thickness indicates gradient. Chalermek Intanagonwiwat, Ramesh Govindan, and Deborah Estrin. Directed diffusion: a scalable and robust communication paradigm for sensor networks. In *Proceedings of the 6th annual international conference on Mobile computing and networking*, MobiCom '00, pages 56–67, New York, NY, USA, 2000. ACM, http://doi.acm.org/10.1145/345910.345920. © 2000 Association for Computing Machinery, Inc. Reprinted by permission

1. First, data is *named* by the values associated with meta-data attributes, e.g. type or location (although we see more sophisticated use of location later). The sensor network's task is described as an *interest* in certain data name(s) at the sink. These interests are diffused through the network, creating *gradients* which describe the strength of the interest in a particular direction—a higher gradient will draw the data more strongly. Note that this differs from SPIN, which assumes that all nodes have an interest in all data—which is true for some scenarios but

not all. The sources indicated are those nodes able to meet this interest at this time, but are not identified at the time the query is created. The interest should also identify a geographic bound on sensors (if they can locate themselves), duration and rate. The initial query sets a low data rate while availability is being explored. The sink may re-broadcast this interest message periodically to capture changes in the network topology, using a time-stamp to identify the message as different from previous broadcasts, so avoiding failure to propagate due to loop detection.

2. Nodes maintain a cache of distinct interests, i.e. those that are different in some property. Duplicate interest messages (due to re-broadcast by nodes with overlapping radio range) or re-broadcasts by the sink are not distinct; while new interests create new entries in the cache. The interest cache entries do not identify the sink, but they do describe a gradient for each neighbour that has expressed that interest to them and the expiry time—note that this requires locally unique but not globally unique node identifiers. A new interest may be sent on to some or all neighbours, thus propagating through the network. Nodes establish an initial gradient for an interest. This identifies a direction and a data rate (or, more generally, a value for that interest in that direction with application determined semantics). Rather than rate, probability might be used to load balance alternative routes.

3. As well as affecting routing an interest identifies data to sense. Not all nodes need to have the same sensing capabilities, but where a node satisfies the interest constraints and is capable it should attempt the required sensing. Some nodes may route an interest from the sink to the interest area, by knowing they are moving data in the correct direction so only participate in the routing even if they have the relevant sensor; other nodes may have other capabilities or be simple routing nodes. The processing will be sensor and application dependent, but may draw on the techniques described in other chapters of this book. Where multiple queries for a type of data exist the highest data rate will be satisfied in the data processing but each interest will be serviced according to the timing constraints given. That interest will result in a periodic message identifying the type, location, time-stamp and other required properties to describe the data. Note that no source node or query identifier is needed.

4. A node receiving data will match it to entries in its interest cache. If no entries exist the message is silently dropped (as in the node at the top of the figures, which has not expressed an interest to the sink so is not forwarded data by the sink); otherwise it is cached. Multiple interests may exist for a given data item, so the data is forwarded to each interested neighbour. The cache allows the node to avoid sending data too quickly where it receives duplicates through multiple paths, and also allows it to combine or interpolate readings to satisfy interests with a different rate.

5. Data eventually arrives at the sink using the initial, low, data rate. It may receive the same data through multiple paths, but will reinforce one neighbour by increasing its gradient using a modified interest message. A simple choice of reinforcement direction is the node first reporting some event, but longer term metrics

can be used to give more stable/less reactive behaviour. This new interest message will match an existing entry in the cache, in neighbour identity and all attributes apart from interest—and so can replace this entry. The receipt of a raised interest also implies that this node must then reinforce one of its neighbours. The data cache is used here to make a choice, using its own local rules—the other nodes in the chain do not know the data path, node status or other interests that node is servicing. As before, a sequence of local interactions give rise to the desired global behaviour without central coordination or even *identical* decisions at each node. Paths should also be negatively reinforced, either by having rates decay or by explicit messages. To have all data reported multiple times would be very inefficient, but unlike the problem of finding shortest paths through a network it is not desirable to reduce the data flow to one path. Node or link failure could quickly cause a periodic data flow to stop or events to be missed. Maintaining some low rate alternative paths, that can easily be reinforced when needed, provides the robustness demanded by sensor network scenarios.

9.5 Querying Sensors

It is possible to view the sensor network as a distributed, self-populating database. In discussing this approach, we shall focus on work at Berkeley (TAG, TinyDB) [12–14], which runs over TinyOS which is widely available as a sensor platform (with integrated processing, unlike Phidgets) and as a simulator.

Programming queries over sensor networks in C is rather low-level and error prone for application developers and end users. A higher level language, such as SQL, with some standard functions relating to sensor networks may provide a simpler interface to deploying the control of processing. Queries can be issued to the network to gather readings, using SQL-like expressions to join streams of data, transform the data (typically into aggregations over nodes or time), and limit the scope of queries. In adopting an SQL like syntax the network is being treated as a database, where columns exist per sensed parameter and rows are only ever appended (as new samples are taken) [13]. An example query might be:

```
SELECT AVG(light), room FROM sensors
WHERE building = science
GROUP BY room
EPOCH DURATION 1min
LIFETIME 24hour
```

9.5.1 Aggregation

Often a sensor network is required to deliver summaries, for instance mapping zones of temperature and humidity in a forest, or counts of traffic per hour in a town. It is not necessary for the sink to have the raw data and generate the summary itself—the network can be involved. Indeed, in-network aggregation can be a useful tool for reducing the communications load and hence extending the network lifetime (if running on batteries). Aggregations include: minimum, maximum, mean, count-if and sum; filtering is also possible, which can exclude some unwanted data altogether.

Computing min and max is generally trivial to implement over a set of nodes: the order of evaluation and different paths through the network do not impact the result. Computing the mean requires that each value is received at most once [13]. This requires that the communications are more structured: forming a tree over the network. The mean is computed at the sink, but communications are limited to a running sum and count of readings. This form gives all readings equal weight without requiring a linear communications pattern or communication of raw data. In [13] aggregation functions are classified, with the measures being:

- Duplicate sensitive, which we've illustrated above—whether duplication of data affects the outcome. It does for count, sum, various averages, and histogram; it does not for max, min and count distinct.
- Exemplary—one or more example values, or summary—processed from all values.
- Monotonic, which determines whether some filtering predicates can be computed in-network using partial state or not.
- Partial state, which determines performance due to the volume of data being moved. This may be equal to the final aggregate, such as count; constant size but not actually the aggregate, such as average computed with a count and sum as above; proportional to the number of distinct values; or proportional in size to some property of the data.

A tree can be formed as follows [13]:

1. The root of the tree is the sink, or the node which forwards data out of the sensor network and to the user. This nodes has *level* zero.
2. The root broadcasts a tree formation message to its neighbours containing its ID and level.
3. A node receiving a tree formation message assigns its level to be the received level plus one and regards the sender as its parent. The message is then re-broadcast to this node's neighbours, substituting its ID and level.
4. A node may receive many tree formation messages, where the network degree is high. Only the first is to be acted on to avoid additional network load.

As this is a flooding algorithm it is expensive, but for many sensor network applications it need only be issued occasionally. In the lifetime of a query the algorithm only needs to be re-run if a child does not hear from a parent beyond a timeout, or if it is expected that nodes of interest will arrive. Aggregations and selection which do not flow down the routing tree cannot be supported.

9.5.2   *Query Deployment*

Queries must be translated to operations on the sensor network: sampling, data processing and communications. We discuss processing in Sect. 9.5.1. Consistent with the local processing approach described for routing above, it is desirable for the query to be distributed across the network in order to reduce network and energy use. The *epoch duration* specified in the example query describes the sample frequency. A fresh "row" should be delivered for each epoch, based on all the devices in the network at that time. This phasing can influence the sample rate (which may be greater than the epoch if a reading requires multiple values at that node to compute). It also determines the communications pattern—which will be to pass data from the leaves of the query tree to their parents, hop by hop to the sink. This is necessary as aggregates may need to combine received and local readings, or at least benefit from sensing multiple readings with one header overhead. This processing limits the minimum epoch duration for a query, while a longer duration with specified communications periods within the epoch allows nodes to go to sleep to save energy.

The temporal structure can be made more flexible, as described in [7]. For instance, events may be used to trigger the delivery of a new row, with processing responding to the event. Consider Hellerstein et al.'s example:

```
ON EVENT bird-detect(loc):
SELECT AVG(light), AVG(temp)
FROM sensors AS s
WHERE dist(s.loc, event.loc) < 10m
SAMPLE INTERVAL 2 s FOR 30 s
```

When a bird is detected data collection and the formation of an aggregate describing the light and temperature is triggered. The sensors used in the aggregate are dependent on the location of the event, so might require nodes to participate in many overlapping cells of event description around the bird detector sensors. Another temporal variation is to report data with varying aggregations at different rates, e.g. reporting min/max data quickly, a mean moderately frequently and a histogram less often. The slower reports may benefit from earlier computations, or ongoing local aggregations at individual nodes. As well as this temporal variation in aggregation other queries might require the identification of isobars or regions of similar conditions. These zones or paths cannot be identified in advance, but to identify them in the network (rather than from raw data at the sink) requires that nodes can route based on sensor values.

9.6   Geographic Knowledge in Networks

Location can be useful in a number of ways in sensor networks:

- It can be part of the data, e.g. the pipe is blocked in the High Street, the fire is in this area.

- It can be used to inform routing, e.g. by helping identify forwarding *towards* a sink. Examples of this approach can be found in [10, 17]. Note also that network connectivity and geographic location are not directly related. It is likely that in any large scale deployment communication barriers or topology will create "holes" where nodes cannot communicate along the shortest spatial path. Even if geographic location informs routing, connectivity is a useful fall-back in these awkward scenarios, where progress towards the destination in the network may require movement away from the destination in space.
- Where nodes have been deployed with no manual configuration or even logging of placement, node maintenance is helped by nodes identifying their location. This may be facilitated by some nodes having GPS, while other nodes may have to compute their approximate location using these special nodes as reference points.

Of course these uses of location can involve different properties of the location system. We shall not repeat Chap. 7 here, but variables in the location service include:

- Location accuracy, for instance GPS has a power burden that many sensor networks cannot support.
- Location update delay, which can be long for a largely static network. The extremes is manual configuration on deployment.
- Absolute positioning, or relative positioning to other nodes, possibly with reference to beacons with more accurately known absolute location. The relative model may be cheaper to produce from radio visibility and signal strength and sufficient for many purposes.

9.7 Summary

In this chapter we have given an overview of sensor networks, presenting core issues including:

- Routing in ad-hoc networks
- Content addressed networks
- Examples of early sensor network protocols, illustrating the use of ad-hoc and content addressing ideas along with localised processing
- The formation of queries over sensor networks
- The use location in these networks

The coverage is necessarily incomplete in a single chapter, but the issues raised are particularly pertinent to the rest of this book and re-illustrate the various techniques considered. The collection and processing of sensor data in an efficient, adaptive manner which reflects the context of nodes, e.g. energy level, location, is an important part of the design of ubiquitous computing infrastructure. Not only do sensor networks require energy aware, self-configuring adaptive protocols with programmable, responsive behaviour—but the collection of this data supports context awareness.

9.8 Suggested Readings

For an accessible introduction to sensor network issues, including power budget and signal processing, one of the following would be useful:

- G. J. Pottie and W. J. Kaiser. Wireless integrated network sensors. *Commun. ACM*, 43:51–58, May 2000
- Paolo Baronti, Prashant Pillai, Vince W.C. Chook, Stefano Chessa, Alberto Gotta, and Y. Fun Hu. Wireless sensor networks: A survey on the state of the art and the 802.15.4 and zigbee standards. *Computer Communications*, 30(7):1655–1695, 2007. Wired/Wireless Internet Communications

At least one of the following classic sensor networking routing papers would be a useful read for some detail on protocols and for the approaches used to study these network algorithms:

- SPIN: Wendi Rabiner Heinzelman, Joanna Kulik, and Hari Balakrishnan. Adaptive protocols for information dissemination in wireless sensor networks. In *Proceedings of the 5th annual ACM/IEEE international conference on Mobile computing and networking*, MobiCom '99, pages 174–185, New York, NY, USA, 1999. ACM
- LEACH: Wendi Rabiner Heinzelman, Anantha Chandrakasan, and Hari Balakrishnan. Energy-efficient communication protocol for wireless microsensor networks. In *HICSS*, 2000
- Directed diffusion: Chalermek Intanagonwiwat, Ramesh Govindan, and Deborah Estrin. Directed diffusion: a scalable and robust communication paradigm for sensor networks. In *Proceedings of the 6th annual international conference on Mobile computing and networking*, MobiCom '00, pages 56–67, New York, NY, USA, 2000. ACM
- PEGASIS: [11]

One of the following papers gives a good discussion on high level query definition and in-network data processing, the latter being a much more substantial journal paper:

- Samuel Madden, Michael J. Franklin, Joseph M. Hellerstein, and Wei Hong. Tag: A tiny aggregation service for ad-hoc sensor networks. In *OSDI*, 2002
- Sam R. Madden and M. Franklin. Fjording the stream: An architecture for queries over streaming sensor data. In *18th International Conference on Data Engineering*, San Jose, CA, USA, 2002
- Samuel Madden, Michael J. Franklin, Joseph M. Hellerstein, and Wei Hong. Tinydb: an acquisitional query processing system for sensor networks. *ACM Trans. Database Syst.*, 30(1):122–173, 2005

9.9 Laboratory Exercises: Introduction to Sensor Nets Simulation

The purpose of this lab is to consider how data may be combined and how relevant data may be identified.

1. Set up sensors to provide multiple readings of the same aspect of context, e.g. light, temperature, noise level. You may use previously collected data to aid in testing and calibration.
2. Consider how the readings from these sensors may be combined through distributed, locally organised computation. Are you planning to indicate events or levels? In both cases, how many different conditions will be described? How does the computation and resulting data differ from the single node local processing you considered in previous chapters?

    The combination of data should lead you to consider various questions on the nature of the sensors and the use of the data:

    - Are there significant offsets in the readings that need to be adjusted for?
    - Do the sensors tend to indicate false positives?
    - How often/under what conditions have you configured each sensor to report? (This is particularly important to consider if you are using an event listener approach rather than polling.)
    - Is a simple average appropriate or will it create strange effects in the data?
    - Is a voting algorithm appropriate?

3. Consider what change your algorithm makes to the number of notifications/rate of variation of levels. To extend this study you might like to compare several approaches. Consider what approaches you will compare: variants on your own, standard models such as flooding and gossiping, or other existing protocols.
4. Consider how a publish-subscribe mechanism would describe a subscription to the values as reported by you. What relations over the data need to be supported?

References

1. Baldoni, R., Querzoni, L., Virgillito, A.: Distributed event routing in publish/subscribe communication systems: a survey. Technical report, Universitá di Roma la Sapienza (2005)
2. Baronti, P., Pillai, P., Chook, V.W.C., Chessa, S., Gotta, A., Hu, Y.F.: Wireless sensor networks: a survey on the state of the art and the 802.15.4 and zigbee standards. Comput. Commun. **30**(7), 1655–1695 (2007). Wired/Wireless Internet Communications
3. Estrin, D., Govindan, R., Heidemann, J., Kumar, S.: Next century challenges: scalable coordination in sensor networks. In: Proceedings of the 5th Annual ACM/IEEE International Conference on Mobile Computing and Networking, MobiCom '99, pp. 263–270. ACM, New York (1999)
4. Fiege, L., Gartner, F., Kasten, O., Zeidler, A.: Supporting mobility in content-based publish/subscribe middleware. In: Endler, M., Schmidt, D. (eds.) Middleware 2003. Lecture Notes in Computer Science, vol. 2672, pp. 998–998. Springer, Berlin (2003)

5. Heinzelman, W.R., Kulik, J., Balakrishnan, H.: Adaptive protocols for information dissemination in wireless sensor networks. In: Proceedings of the 5th Annual ACM/IEEE International Conference on Mobile Computing and Networking, MobiCom '99, pp. 174–185. ACM, New York (1999)

6. Heinzelman, W.R., Chandrakasan, A., Balakrishnan, H.: Energy-efficient communication protocol for wireless microsensor networks. In: HICSS, 2000

7. Hellerstein, J.M., Hong, W., Madden, S., Stanek, K.: Beyond average: toward sophisticated sensing with queries. In: Zhao, F., Guibas, L.J. (eds.) IPSN. Lecture Notes in Computer Science, vol. 2634, pp. 63–79. Springer, Berlin (2003)

8. Intanagonwiwat, C., Govindan, R., Estrin, D.: Directed diffusion: a scalable and robust communication paradigm for sensor networks. In: Proceedings of the 6th Annual International Conference on Mobile Computing and Networking MobiCom '00, pp. 56–67. ACM, New York (2000)

9. Johnson, D.B., Maltz, D.A., Broch, J.: In: Perkins, C.E. (ed.) DSR: The Dynamic Source Routing Protocol for Multi-Hop Wireless Ad Hoc Networks, Chap. 5, pp. 139–172. Addison-Wesley, Reading (2001)

10. Kim, Y.-J., Govindan, R., Karp, B., Shenker, S.: Geographic routing made practical. In: NSDI. USENIX, Berkeley (2005)

11. Lindsey, S., Raghavendra, C., Sivalingam, K.M.: Data gathering algorithms in sensor networks using energy metrics. IEEE Trans. Parallel Distrib. Syst. **13**(9), 924–935 (2002)

12. Madden, S.R., Franklin, M.: Fjording the stream: an architecture for queries over streaming sensor data. In: 18th International Conference on Data Engineering, San Jose, CA, USA, 2002

13. Madden, S., Franklin, M.J., Hellerstein, J.M., Hong, W.: Tag: a tiny aggregation service for ad-hoc sensor networks. In: OSDI, 2002

14. Madden, S., Franklin, M.J., Hellerstein, J.M., Hong, W.: Tinydb: an acquisitional query processing system for sensor networks. ACM Trans. Database Syst. **30**(1), 122–173 (2005)

15. Perkins, C.E., Royer, E.M.: Ad-hoc on-demand distance vector routing. In: Mobile Computing Systems and Applications, IEEE Workshop on. IEEE Computer Society, Washington (1999)

16. Pottie, G.J., Kaiser, W.J.: Wireless integrated network sensors. Commun. ACM **43**, 51–58 (2000)

17. Rao, A., Papadimitriou, C.H., Shenker, S., Stoica, I.: Geographic routing without location information. In: Johnson, D.B., Joseph, A.D., Vaidya, N.H. (eds.) MOBICOM, pp. 96–108. ACM, New York (2003)

18. Szewczyk, R., Osterweil, E., Polastre, J., Hamilton, M., Mainwaring, A.M., Estrin, D.: Habitat monitoring with sensor networks. Commun. ACM **47**(6), 34–40 (2004)

Index

D. Chalmers, *Sensing and Systems in Pervasive Computing*,
Undergraduate Topics in Computer Science,
DOI 10.1007/978-0-85729-841-6, © Springer-Verlag London Limited 2011